SUGAR BUSTERS!™
Quick & Easy Cookbook

Books by H. Leighton Steward, Morrison C. Bethea, M.D.,
Sam S. Andrews, M.D., and Luis A. Balart, M.D.

SUGAR BUSTERS!™: Cut Sugar to Trim Fat

SUGAR BUSTERS!™ Shopper's Guide

SUGAR BUSTERS!™ Quick & Easy Cookbook

SUGAR BUSTERS!™
Quick & Easy
Cookbook

H. LEIGHTON STEWARD
MORRISON C. BETHEA, M.D.
SAM S. ANDREWS, M.D.
LUIS A. BALART, M.D.

BALLANTINE BOOKS • NEW YORK

Dedicated to those who think enough of themselves, their families, and their friends to make the reasonable dietary and lifestyle changes to help ensure a better future regarding their health, weight, and self-esteem.

Contents

Foreword   ix

I   Introduction   1

II   The SUGAR BUSTERS! Pantry   17

III   Using Spices, Herbs, and Seasonings   36

IV   Breakfast   56

V   Lunch   86

VI   Dinner   148

VII   Vegetables   213

VIII   Appetizers and Hors d'oeuvres   287

IX   Salad Dressings, Sauces, and
       Stocks   304

X   Snacks   328

XI   Desserts   331

XII   Holiday Menus   345

XIII   Setting the Record Straight   371

Index   378

Foreword

The SUGAR BUSTERS! lifestyle was first chronicled in an author-published trade paperback book entitled *SUGAR BUSTERS! Cut Sugar to Trim Fat* in 1995. It was authored by a Fortune 500 CEO with a Master of Science degree and three medical doctors with specialties that bear on providing good health. Easily translated into knowledge and experience regarding the importance of nutrition in either enhancing or negatively affecting your health, their areas of expertise include cardiovascular and thoracic surgery (heart surgeon), endocrinology (gland specialist, which includes the pancreas), and gastroenterology-hepatology (liver specialist).

The "dietary lifestyle" proposed is a simple way of eating that allows you to eat most foods in normal quantities, possibly even in larger quantities than you presently consume. You can have three full meals a day and even appropriate snacks. There are only a few things you cannot consume on this diet. They are the carbohydrates that cause an intense secretion of insulin, which causes your body to store excess sugar as fat. These carbohydrates include red and white potatoes, corn, white rice, highly processed grain products, beets, carrots, and, of course, the refined sugars and products made with such sugars. Beyond that, most foods are acceptable!

How much success have people had with this way of eating? While no rigorous clinical trials have been conducted, more than 95 percent of respondents have reported losing significant quantities of weight. Very importantly, respondents have experienced an average 15 percent reduction in cholesterol levels, significantly lower levels of blood serum triglycerides, improvement in reducing or eliminating indigestion, improvement in those suffering with episodes of hypoglycemia (low blood sugar), a reduction in the number of or elimination of migraine headaches, and a sustained pick-up in energy level. Very significantly, nearly all diabetics have experienced a reduction in blood sugar levels, with most requiring less medication and many requiring none at all.

Now, after having observed the tremendous success people have had following this lifestyle as well as receiving thousands of testimonials regarding the success others have had, the authors want to respond to the ever-present requests that they provide recipes to help people easily follow this beneficial way of eating.

This cookbook features recipes that, while healthful, savory, and filling, can be prepared quickly and easily to help you continue to experience these beneficial health effects and to help you who never seem to have enough time to cook meals requiring an hour or more to assemble. It also provides tips on how to plan ahead and prepare, or simply get some ingredients "stockpiled," some items marinated, or a pot of beans going that will make it convenient later in the week to cook some great 20-minute dishes.

SUGAR BUSTERS! Quick & Easy Cookbook is designed to be user-friendly. It is divided into three primary sections that consist of recipes for breakfast, lunch, and dinner. Some overlap occurs, mainly between lunch and dinner recipes, but to facilitate preparation of a meal on short notice, the book is organized so if you want a recipe for a quick lunch menu, you shouldn't have to thumb through the entire book to find a suitable selection. Also included are other regular chapters on stocking your pantry, using spices, herbs, and seasonings, vegetables, appetizers, desserts, etc., as well as frequent tips on how to vary recipes to your taste or on what the food items in your chosen recipe contain in the way of beneficial nutrients.

The SUGAR BUSTERS! lifestyle is a logical, practical, and highly flexible eating plan and contains no requirements to count, weigh, and measure that cause so many diets to be discarded. Just as the original SUGAR BUSTERS! book enabled folks across the country to lose weight and feel better while enjoying foods they had denied themselves for years, including fabulous restaurant meals, the *SUGAR BUSTERS! Quick & Easy Cookbook* will show you how to re-create many all-time favorite dishes in your kitchen and provide you with the know-how to create and adapt your own recipes in accordance with your own taste and the healthy SUGAR BUSTERS! way of eating.

Finally, for those of you confused by the various comments quoted in the media that are critical of certain aspects of this way of eating, a chapter is provided to set the record straight and put you at ease regarding these ofttime self-serving or curiously uninformed comments.

The authors would like to acknowledge Barry Bluestein and Kevin Morrisey who tested the recipes, organized the recipes in a consistent pattern of presentation, and even contributed some recipes of their own that fit nicely into the SUGAR BUSTERS! lifestyle.

1 | Introduction

The underlying principles of the SUGAR BUSTERS! lifestyle can be found in medical textbooks. Despite the understandable confusion you may have about the role of refined and natural sugars (carbohydrates) in providing fat to the body's fat cells, the undeniable fact is that most sugar you eat is converted to fat in your body. Your confusion lies in the fact that some (by all means not all!) nutritionists and spokespersons for the nutrition or sugar industry associations make public statements like: "That is absurd! Everybody knows that sugar does not turn to fat!," or "The only way you can get diabetes is through heredity!," or "Well, your diet certainly won't keep the weight off long term!" So yes, you have had a right to be confused. Some nutritional "theories" do appear to make sense, but often they are inconsistent with basic physiological facts or the results of controlled studies. SUGAR BUSTERS! relies upon established medical facts or carefully controlled study results.

How Sugar Causes Your Body to Store Fat

The hormone that signals your body's cells to be receptive to the storage of fat is insulin, which is why it is so often referred to as the fat storage hormone. When you consume sugar, either from the refined types or the natural carbohydrates you eat, the rising blood sugar triggers the release of insulin. Insulin plays the key role in driving blood sugar back down to its normal level. So, an obvious answer to help control your body's storage of fat is to modulate downward (reduce) the amount of insulin you cause your pancreas to secrete. To do that, simply do not eat as much sugar, especially those that cause your blood sugar to rise so rapidly. When you do eat sugar, get it primarily from high-fiber carbohydrates like those that are included in many of the recipes contained in this book.

The Glycemic Index Can Help You Distinguish Good Carbohydrates from Bad

What carbohydrates should you avoid? A carbohydrate's ability to cause a rise in your blood sugar to a given level over a certain period of time can be expressed as that food's glycemic index. On our glycemic scale, glucose, or essentially pure sugar, is set at a value of 100. For exactly the same number of grams of a food, such as a potato, bean, orange, etc., a blood sugar response can be measured and the value plotted in relation to that of glucose (100).

Glycemic indexes for many common foods are provided in Table 1 beginning on page 4. Simply try to avoid those with a high glycemic index like a white potato (80 to 95), and eat more of those like beans (30 to 40), green vegetables (<15), etc., as a source of the necessary sugar your body needs for its immediate and future energy requirements.

The high-fiber carbohydrates are generally the low-glycemic carbohydrates. The presence of fiber in a carbohydrate slows its digestion and absorption and, therefore, its ability to "spike" your blood sugar, and this means it also will not "spike" your insulin! We have all heard of the benefits of high-fiber diets for possibly reducing the incidence of colon cancer and cardiovascular diseases. High-fiber vegetables also provide larger quantities of the antioxidant vitamins than do most of the low-fiber vegetables.[1] These benefits go hand in hand with the SUGAR BUSTERS! recommendation of eating the correct, high-fiber carbohydrates.

Table 1: Glycemic Index

Grains, Breads, and Cereals
High

Instant rice	90
White pretzels	85
Corn Flakes	85
Rice Krispies	80
Rice cakes	80
Grape Nuts Flakes	80
White bread	75
French bread	75

[1]Oral comments by Dr. Margaret Spitz, Professor and Chair of Department of Epidemiology of Immunology at M.D. Anderson Cancer Hospital in Houston, Texas, on October 15, 1998, San Antonio, Texas.

Corn	75
Corn chips	75
Graham crackers	75
Regular crackers	75
White bagel	75
Total cereal	75
Cheerios	75
Puffed wheat	75
Croissant	70
Corn meal	70
White rice	70
Taco shells	70
Cream of Wheat	70
Shredded wheat	70
Melba toast	70
Millet	70
Grape-Nuts cereal	65
Instant regular oatmeal	65
Whole-wheat crackers	65
Nutri•Grain cereal	65
Stoned Wheat Thins	65
Regular pasta	65
Couscous	60
Basmati rice	60
Spaghetti, white	60

Introduction

Moderate

Muesli, no sugar added	55
Pita bread, regular	55
Rye sourdough	55
Wild rice	55
Brown rice	55
Oatmeal	55
Special K	55
Whole-grain pumpernickel	50
Cracked-wheat bulgur bread	50
High percent cracked-wheat bread	50
Whole rice	50
Oat and bran bread	50
Sponge cake	45
Pita bread, stone-ground	45
Wheat grain	45
Barley grain	45
Whole-grain pasta	45
All-Bran, no sugar added	45
Whole-meal spaghetti	40

Low

Rye grain	35

Vegetables

<u>**High**</u>

Baked potato	95
Parsnips	95
Carrots	85
French fries	80
Beets	75

<u>**Moderate**</u>

Sweet potatoes	55
Yams	50
Green peas	45
Black-eyed peas	40

<u>**Low**</u>

Dried beans, lentils	30–40
Pinto beans	40
Green beans	40
Chick peas	35
Lima beans	30
Black beans	30
Butter beans	30
Kidney beans	30
Soy beans	15
Green vegetables	0–15

Introduction

Fruits

High

Watermelon	70
Pineapple	65
Raisins	65
Ripe bananas	60

Moderate

Mango	50
Kiwi	50
Grapes	50
Plantain banana	45
Pears	45
Peaches	40
Plums	40
Apples	40
Oranges	40

Low

Apricots, dried	30
Grapefruit	25
Cherries	25
Tomatoes	15
Apricots, fresh	10

Introduction

Dairy Products

High

Ice cream, premium	60

Low

Yogurt, with added fruit	35
Milk, whole	>30
Milk, skimmed	<30
Yogurt, plain, no sugar	15

Miscellaneous

High

Maltose (as in beer)	105
Glucose	100
Pretzels	80
Honey	75
Refined sugar	75
Popcorn	55

Low

Nuts	15–30
Peanuts	15

This Diet Is Outstanding for Diabetics

The SUGAR BUSTERS! lifestyle is particularly effective for helping to control diabetes. Diabetics have been told to eliminate things like table sugar and candy, but few have been told that high-glycemic foods like a baked potato or slices of white bread cause their bodies to need as much or more insulin as an equal amount of table sugar or candy! By simply eliminating a few high-glycemic carbohydrates, diabetics can lead a much healthier and more pleasant life.

The SUGAR BUSTERS! lifestyle also can help reduce the risk of expectant mothers developing gestational diabetes. While gestational diabetes is generally confined to the time of the pregnancy, it puts the mother and her unborn child at a greater risk of developing diabetes later on in life. Furthermore, switching to low-glycemic, high-fiber carbohydrates can help a new mother safely lose the extra pounds gained during pregnancy.

You Can Add Years and Quality to Your Children's Lives

Obesity in children has doubled in just the last two decades. Fat children predominantly become fat adults and 60 percent of fat children experience health problems directly related to their being overweight. For example, Type II (adult onset) diabetes in children has increased dramatically. Also, recent pathological studies have indicated that arteriosclerosis starts early, even during teenage years.

What more do you need to convince you that the high-glycemic carbohydrate, low-fiber diets you and your children have been consuming are the wrong way to nourish your bodies? Well, there is more. A limited study on 12 obese boys, reported in *Pediatrics* in March 1999,[2] found that when the boys were fed high-glycemic carbohydrates at breakfast and lunch, they chose to eat much more food at the next meal than when the same boys were fed an equal amount of low-glycemic carbohydrates for breakfast and lunch.

[2]Drs. Ludwig, Majzoub, Al-Zahrani, and Dallal, et al, Division of Endocrinology, Department of Medicine, Tufts University, Boston, Massachusetts.

So if you have not been inclined to follow the SUGAR BUSTERS! lifestyle yourself, please serve it in your household for the sake of your children's health and well-being.

Carbohydrate-Protein-Fat Ratio

While many of our individual recipes do contain somewhat higher levels of protein and fat than you may currently be consuming, we would expect that when accompanied by the higher-fiber vegetables, salads, whole-grain breads, etc., your meals should average about 40 percent correct carbohydrates, 30 percent protein, and 30 percent fat just as they do in the 14-day meal plan in our book, SUGAR BUSTERS!. The 40-30-30 proportion of carbohydrates, protein, and fat can be skewed toward even more carbohydrates (greater than 50 percent carbohydrates) if you are consuming primarily low-glycemic carbohydrates.

Let us not leave the discussion of proportions without discussing the consumption of saturated fats. This is an area where moderation is the wisest choice. We do not say a slightly higher proportion of consumed saturated fats will necessarily cause you to gain weight, but it will put you at a higher risk for developing cardiovascular disease. So don't just think thin, think thin and healthy, and trim those meats. Also avoid frequent use of large quantities of cream and other sources of saturated fats.

Portion Sizes and Calories

Proper portion size is important. While the role of calories in weight gain has been dramatically oversimplified and misunderstood by those who would construct all kinds of theories about how your body reacts to "a calorie," eating too much of almost anything will result in weight gain for a majority of our population. Some of the nutritional "theorists" believe that your body's metabolism reacts to a calorie, whatever its source, as if your body were a mindless steam engine. Your body's reaction to a protein-rich meal vs. a carbohydrate-rich meal and the resulting insulin secretion is well laid out in the *Williams Textbook on Endocrinology* by Doctors Wilson and Foster.[3] So one calorie is not necessarily like another calorie in the way it affects your

[3]Wilson, J. D., and D. W. Foster, *Williams Textbook of Endocrinology*, 8th ed., Philadelphia; W. B. Saunders, 1992.

body's metabolism, including weight gain or loss or even cholesterol generation. But, sadly, the calorie theory and similar nutritional dogma permeates most of what you continue to be bombarded with every day in the various media.

We have tried to approach portion or meal size in a very straightforward and user-friendly manner. Eat three platefuls a day with appropriate snacks in between. Do not eat three platefuls at one time and do not stack the plate as high as your fork! While some people can get away with consuming large quantities of moderate-to low-glycemic foods, many of us cannot. Also, while some even can consume large quantities of high-glycemic foods without gaining weight, many of these individuals will exhibit other health problems associated with high levels of insulin, such as elevated cholesterol levels (hypercholesterolemia) or elevated triglyceride levels (hyperlipidemia), diabetes, or premature cardiovascular disease.

Liquid Consumption Is Also Important

Liquids are very important to your body (which happens to be 57 percent water!). Drink several glasses of water per day. Fresh juices at snack time are also okay. Total liquid intake should be at least 45 to 50 ounces. Dehydration is not good for you, can make you feel lousy, and, in the extreme, make you pass out. But do not drink a significant amount of any liquid during a meal. Consumption of large quantities of liquids at mealtime only serves to dilute the digestive juices in your stomach and slow the normal digestion of your food.

The SUGAR BUSTERS! Quick & Easy Cookbook

The recipes included in this book have been originally created or collected by the authors over a period of years. Many have come from old family recipes. Several are simply modifications of old tried-and-true recipes wherein some original ingredients that are not consistent with a healthy SUGAR BUSTERS! lifestyle were modified to correct the inconsistency and have been done in a way as to not significantly alter the flavor. In some cases, the modifications have even enhanced the flavor. We are particularly appreciative of those who have volunteered to share their appropriate recipes and who have agreed to have them placed in this cookbook. We hope one thing becomes very apparent to all of you; most recipes (not all) can be modified to be acceptable SUGAR BUSTERS! type recipes. Once you get the hang of it, we hope you will have as much fun in the kitchen as we are having.

SUGAR BUSTERS! Products Now Available in Various Areas

Many of you are frustrated by the lack of low-glycemic products in the marketplace and have written to ask SUGAR BUSTERS! to develop some "legal" items. In the following chapter, Table 3, page 31, sets forth the products that are available in various areas as of the summer of 1999. The areas of distribution are expanding rapidly. If you are interested, please consider this list of products in stocking your SUGAR BUSTERS! pantry.

II | The SUGAR BUSTERS! Pantry

Stocking your pantry, freezer, and refrigerator with products that help facilitate the SUGAR BUSTERS! way of eating will pave the way for quick and easy meal preparation. The following is a sampling of acceptable foods that are used in the *SUGAR BUSTERS! Quick & Easy Cookbook* recipes, along with some that you should avoid. You'll note when shopping the SUGAR BUSTERS! way that the best supermarket choices are around the perimeter of the store rather than in the center, where the processed foods are located. There are a lot of surprising sources of blood sugar–elevating carbohydrates in canned goods; always compare nutritional labels among brands and select those products containing the least amount of added sugar and in no case more than 3 grams of "sugars" per serving.

Acceptable Vegetables and Miscellaneous Produce

(Remember that fresh is always best, followed by frozen, and then canned.)

Artichokes

Avocadoes

Dried beans of all kinds

Green beans

Broccoli

Cabbages

Cauliflower

Celery

Cilantro

Cucumbers

Eggplant

Garlic

Ginger

Green onions

Greens

Fresh herbs of all kinds

Lentils

Lettuces

Mushrooms of all kinds
Okra
Onions
Flat-leaf and curly parsley
Peas
Bell peppers
Chili peppers
Spinach
Squash
Sweet potatoes, in moderation
Tomatoes
Zucchini
Avoid: beets, carrots, corn, parsnips, red and
     white potatoes (including French fries),
     turnips, frozen or canned vegetables with
     sugar added

Acceptable Fruit

Apples
Apricots
Berries of all kinds
Cantaloupes
Cherries
Grapes
Honeydew melons

Kiwis, except very ripe

Lemons

Limes

Nectarines

Oranges

Peaches

Pears

Plums

Tangerines

Avoid: ripe bananas, pineapples, raisins,
watermelon, frozen fruit with sugar added,
canned fruit in syrup

Acceptable Meats

Canadian bacon

Lean bacon (not sugar cured)

Lean ground beef

Trimmed lean beef

Chicken

Ham (not sugar cured)

Lean trimmed lamb

Trimmed pork

Quail and other game birds

Turkey

Trimmed veal

Avoid: fatty cuts of beef and lamb, sugar-cured
ham and bacon, cold cuts with "sugars" added

Acceptable Seafood

Crab of all kinds
Crayfish
Fish of all kinds, especially healthful are cold
water fish for omega-3 fatty acids
Oysters
Bay and sea scallops
Shrimp
Avoid: breaded fish, sugar-cured fish

Acceptable Dairy Products

Butter, in moderation
Block and grated cheese
Cream cheese (preferably reduced-fat)
Goat cheese
Eggs
Egg substitute
Milk (preferably low-fat)
Sour cream (preferably reduced-fat)
Yogurt with no sugar added (preferably low-fat
or nonfat)

Avoid: yogurt with sugar or maltodextrin
added, excessive consumption of high-fat
dairy products

Acceptable Baked Goods

Stone-ground, whole-wheat bagels
Stone-ground, whole-wheat breads
Whole-grain breads
Avoid: breads made with refined flour and more
than one gram of sugar, most pastries; and
just do not eat too much bread of any kind!

Acceptable Canned Goods, Garnishes, Condiments, etc.

Artichoke bottoms and hearts
Most beans
Beef broth
Chicken broth
Green chilies
Hearts of palm
Prepared horseradish
Ketchup, in moderation, if consumed with
protein
Reduced-fat mayonnaise

Mustards
Canola oil
Olive oil
Oil sprays
Olives
Plain and pickled jalapeño peppers
Roasted red peppers
Dill pickles
Salsas
Hollandaise sauce
Hot sauce
Reduced-sodium soy sauce
Steak sauces
Worcestershire sauce
Spreadable fruit (no sugar added)
Tomato juice
Tomato purée
Tomato sauce (no sugar added)
Tomatoes
Tuna
Balsamic vinegar
Cider vinegar
White vinegar
Avoid: baked beans, mayonnaise, sweet
   pickles, sugar-sweetened jams, jellies, and
   preserves

Acceptable Dry Packaged Products

High bran cereals with no sugar added (such as
All-Bran Extra Fiber, Oat Bran, and Shredded
Wheat 'N Bran)
Whole-grain cereals with no sugar added
Whole-grain crackers (such as whole-grain
crispbread or wafers and rye crackers)
Whole-wheat croutons
Stone-ground, whole-wheat flour
Fructose and artificial sweeteners
Whole, rolled, or steel-cut oats
Whole-wheat pastas
Stone-ground pitas
Brown rice (not instant)
Brown basmati rice
Whole-wheat tortillas
Avoid: cold cereals with sugar added (most),
Cream of Wheat, flavored instant hot cereals,
regular crackers, all-purpose and other
enriched flour, products made with enriched
flour, sugar, significant amounts of white
pastas, white rice, and risotto.

"Acceptable" Alcohols—in Moderation

Red wine (preferably dry)—provides a
    beneficial cardiovascular effect
White wine (preferably dry), including
    champagne
Liquor with water, soda, or sugar-free mixers
Avoid: Beer (Beer bellies are there for a
    reason—the gylcemic index on maltose is
    greater than glucose), sweet after-dinner
    wines or liqueurs, and liquor with mixers
    containing sugar
Note: We are not encouraging you to drink al-
cohol. Realistically, however, we know many
people do consume alcohol, and we have simply
listed those most acceptable and those to avoid.

Beans, the Better Choice

Beans are a great source of carbohydrates, protein, and fiber and are a staple of the SUGAR
BUSTERS! lifestyle. Beans can be the primary
substitute for the red and white potatoes, white
rice, and the corn you were formerly eating.

While dried beans cannot be adequately cooked
in 20 or 30 minutes, we have included recipes

for beans because they can be cooked with little supervision, and beans keep well when refrigerated for at least a week. Beans provide the basic ingredients for various soups. The recipes provided in this cookbook are very basic and often similar, if not identical, to those provided on the commercial packages of dried beans.

Gastronomically, most beans are easily enhanced by the addition of your favorite salsas or, in the case of lentils, by adding a few dashes of a commercial pepper and vinegar sauce. Most commercial salsas contain little to no added sugar.

The glycemic index or blood sugar stimulating effect of beans increases as cooking time increases and the beans soften, so we encourage you to try and cook your beans until they are only "al dente" or still a little bit firm. Many cookbook recipes recommend cooking practices that cause the beans to become very soft, if not mushy, and thus, more highly glycemic. If you try bean recipes from another cookbook, try reducing the cooking time by about 10 percent to get a "better for your belly" result.

Home-cooked dried beans taste much better than canned, are more nutritious, and often have a lower glycemic index as well. If you do need to use canned beans in a pinch, know that a 15-ounce can is the equivalent of 1½ to 2 cups cooked dried beans, depending on the variety of bean.

To soak dried beans (a necessary first step): Put picked-over beans into a large bowl. Add sufficient water to cover by 2 inches and let soak overnight at room temperature, then drain. You can also quick-soak the beans. Put them into a large pot and add water to cover by 1½ to 2 inches. Bring to a boil and boil for 5 minutes. Cover, remove from the heat, and let sit for 1 hour, then drain.

To cook about 1 pound (2 to 3 cups, depending upon the variety of bean) soaked dried beans: Combine the beans and about 8 cups water in a large pot. Bring to a boil. Cover, reduce the heat to low, and simmer for about 1 hour, until the beans are tender. Every 1 cup dried beans will yield about 2½ cups cooked beans.

Roasts

Another feature that can be cooked and stock-piled for the week is a nice large roast. Roasts are cooked slowly (and fairly effortlessly) and are usually well done but still moist throughout. Accordingly, roasts can be reheated and eaten again as a main dish, as bites for hors d'oeuvres, or even in an omelet for breakfast.

Basic Broths (Stocks)

Broths are easy and rewarding, since homemade broth is always better than canned. You'll use it constantly—even in place of some of the water in the recipe above to cook beans. Make a big batch when you have time and freeze measured portions in heavy-duty plastic freezer storage bags. With slight variations, this simple formula will work for chicken, beef, or fish broth. You can often get the needed bones or carcasses from your butcher or fish market. If you need to substitute canned broth for homemade, use one 14½-ounce can for every 1¾ cups broth.

3 quarts water
3 yellow onions, quartered
3 cloves garlic, mashed (optional)
3 stalks celery, chopped
About 6 pounds chicken neck, back, leg, or

wing bones with meat scraps, browned, or about 6 pounds beef with lean meat scraps, browned, or 3 to 4 pounds fish carcasses (without heads) and/or shrimp or crab shells

Combine the water, onions, garlic, celery, and chicken bones or beef bones or fish carcasses and/or shells in a large stockpot. Bring to a boil, then lower the heat to maintain a bare simmer. Cook up to 4 hours (but only about 1 hour for fast-cooking fish stock). Strain and refrigerate. For chicken or beef broth, skim congealed fat from the surface before using.

Oils

Every cooking oil is composed of varying amounts of the three different types of fat: saturated, polyunsaturated, and monounsaturated. Saturated fats are usually from animal sources, such as butter and bacon grease, and are solid at room temperature. There are also vegetable sources of saturated fats, such as palm oil, coconut oil, and cocoa butter. Saturated fats are associated with an increased incidence of heart disease and elevated blood cholesterol levels.

Polyunsaturated and monounsaturated fats

are usually from vegetable, nut, or seed sources and are liquid at room temperature. Some poly-unsaturated fats, linoleic and alpha-linoleic acid, in a limited amount, are absolutely necessary in our diets for good health. These fats may help lower blood cholesterol levels. Oils that are good sources of polyunsaturated fats are rapeseed (canola), safflower, sunflower, soybean, corn, cottonseed, and sesame. Good sources of monounsaturated fats are olive, canola, and peanut oils.

In choosing a cooking oil, select one low in saturated fat, moderate in good polyunsaturated fats, and relatively high in monounsaturated fats. Table 2 below will assist you in making a good choice. We recommend canola and olive oils. Spray oils are usually acceptable since they have a vegetable source and are unsaturated. Remember that heating polyunsaturated and monounsaturated oils adds hydrogen, converting them to saturated oils. Do not save or reuse oils after they have been heated. This is why foods cooked in fast food restaurants, where often oils are reheated constantly during the day, are not a good choice.

Table 2: Comparison of Dietary Fats

DIETARY FAT	FATTY ACID CONTENT NORMALIZED TO 100 PER CENT			
Canola oil	7%	21%	11%	61%
Safflower oil	10%	76%	Trace	14%
Sunflower oil	12%	71%	1%	16%
Corn oil	13%	57%	1%	29%
Olive oil	15%	9%	1%	75%
Soybean oil	15%	54%	8%	23%
Peanut oil	19%	33%	Trace	48%
Cottonseed oil	27%	54%	Trace	19%
Lard*	43%	9%	1%	47%
Beef tallow*	48%	2%	1%	49%
Palm oil*	51%	10%	Trace	39%
Butterfat*	68%	3%	1%	28%
Coconut oil*	91%		2%	7%

*Cholesterol Content (mg/Tbsp): Lard 12; Beef tallow 14; Butterfat 33. No cholesterol in any vegetable-based oil.
Source: POS Pilot Plant Corporation, Saskatoon, Saskatchewan, Canada June 1994

■ SATURATED FAT

□ MONOUNSATURATED FAT

POLYUNSATURATED FAT
■ Linoleic Acid
□ Alpha-Linolenic Acid
(An Omega-3 Fatty Acid)

Canola Council of Canada

Table 3: SUGAR BUSTERS!™ (Authors' Choice Brand) Products

Product	Location Available
Tomato basil soup	Many major cities nationwide*, especially in the Southeast, Texas, and California
Chili with beans	" " "
Black bean soup	" " "
Chicken cacciatore	" " "
Lentil soup	" " "
7 Bean soup	" " "

The Sugar Busters! Pantry

The Sugar Busters! Pantry

Turkey & sausage gumbo	"	"	"
Bread			
Rustic loaf	Many major cities nationwide*, especially in the Southeast, Texas, and California		
Multigrain loaf	"	"	"
Baguette	"	"	"
French bread/Po-boy	"	"	"
Baguettine	"	"	"
Pistolette	"	"	"
Dinner rolls	"	"	"
Pita bread	The Southeast, Texas, and California		
Hot dog rolls	"	"	"
Hamburger rolls	"	"	"
Rye bread	"	"	"
Sourdough bread	"	"	"
Blueberry muffin	"	"	"
Bran muffin	"	"	"
Apple nut muffin	"	"	"
Sweet potato muffin	"	"	"
Parmesan herb muffin	"	"	"
Meats**			
Oven roast turkey	The Southeast, Texas, and California		

Smoked turkey	" " "
Smoked ham	" " "
Roast beef	" " "
Entrées & Salads	
Chicken salad	The Southeast, Texas, and California
Tuna salad	" " "
Salad Dressings	
Blue cheese	Many major cities nationwide*, especially in the Southeast, Texas, and California
French	" " "
Thousand island	" " "
Ranch	" " "
Italian	" " "
Condiments	
Mayonnaise	Many major cities nationwide*, especially in the Southeast, Texas, and California
Pastas (Dry)	
Angel hair	Many major cities nationwide*, especially in the Southeast, Texas, and California

Spaghetti   //   //   //

Fettuccine   //   //   //

Lasagna   //   //   //

Spirals   //   //   //

Egg noodles   //   //   //

In Development†

Lasagna

Stuffed bell peppers

Additional salad dressings

Ketchup

Regular barbecue sauce

Spicy barbecue sauce

Breakfast cereals

Stone-ground, whole-wheat flour

Ice creams

High cocoa chocolates

Bacon

The following grocery chains are currently carrying some or all of listed products but may not yet be carrying them in all stores, or for the nationwide chain stores, in all areas of the United States. If your local stores are not carrying a product or product line and you would like to have it available, simply request that the store manager stock the product in the future. The

manager can contact Boudreaux Foods, 8224
Maple Street, New Orleans, Louisiana 70118, or
by calling (504) 866-9500.

Albertsons

Kroger

Super Kmart

Winn Dixie

Sav-A-Center

Jittney Jungle

Bruno's—Alabama and Georgia

Randalls

HEB

Brookshire Brothers

Brookshire Groceries

Bi-Lo

Rice Food Markets

Market Basket

Cub Foods

Piggly Wiggly

*Currently available in a limited number of
stores; expanding monthly.

**Sugar-free meats.

†May be available as of time of publication.

III | Using Spices, Herbs, and Seasonings

Oils, spices, and seasonings facilitate cooking and enhance the flavor of your foods. Knowledge of these ingredients is not only helpful but also healthy because some oils are heart-healthy and others are not. In keeping with the SUGAR BUSTERS! concept, this section is included to assist you in making better choices when preparing your favorite recipes.

There is considerable variation among regions of the country, cultures, and individuals regarding spices and seasonings. In New Orleans, food is generally preferred "spicy." However, the best advice is to try different spices and season to your taste. Spices have little, if any, nutritional value. Fortunately, spices pack a big punch for adding flavor but have essentially no effect on causing a glycemic or blood sugar–raising response. This gives you the opportunity to freely use spices from all over the world to add tremendous flavor to the SUGAR BUSTERS! dishes you prepare or, if preferred, you can add little or no flavoring and simply enjoy the subtle taste of the meat or vegetable itself.

Eating food the way your ancient ancestors ate food, i.e., more whole grains and no refined sugar, makes all kind of metabolic sense, but, flavor-wise, your ancestors were restricted to the use of whatever herbs, spices, and seasonings happened to grow in their local area. Spices, herbs, and seasonings are now available from all over the world. So when you go to your spice rack or refrigerator tonight, just think how much better you can make that vegetable or piece of fish taste than could your relatives of just a hundred years ago. Don't waste the opportunity; get creative and satisfy your taste buds completely.

Unlike spices commonly used, seasonings, such as onions and garlic, do contain significant nutritive value and can even generate a low to modest glycemic response. However, since the response is limited, we have included these seasoning vegetables in the list of spices to make it easier for you to find your choice of flavor enhancers.

To assist you in discovering the best way to truly enhance the flavor of your foods, the following tables are presented in two user-friendly ways. First, you can look up what meat or vegetable you plan to prepare and quickly see what spices or seasonings have been used historically to enhance your choice. Secondly, you may have some fresh herbs, spices, or seasonings in your refrigerator or in your garden and be wondering what kind of dishes they would best enhance. Accordingly, we have also provided a list of spices and seasonings followed by what foods they complement best.

Remember that old, dried-out spices have usually lost most of their flavor. Keep your spices in tightly sealed jars, away from the light and stored away from the heat.

Table 4: Spices, Herbs, and Seasonings that Complement Various Foods

Meat	Spices, Herbs, and Seasonings
Beef*	Basil, cumin, garlic, horseradish, marjoram, onion, parsley, black

pepper, white pepper, rosemary, sage, savory, thyme.

Chicken	Basil, celery, chervil, curry powder, dill, garlic, ginger, lemon juice, marjoram, nutmeg, onion, oregano, paprika, parsley, black pepper, cayenne pepper, white pepper, rosemary, saffron, sage, savory, sesame seeds, tarragon, thyme, turmeric.
Ham*	Cinnamon, cloves, ginger, mustard, tarragon.
Hamburger	Basil, celery seeds, garlic, marjoram, onion, oregano, paprika, parsley, black pepper, cayenne pepper, white pepper, sage, thyme.
Lamb*	Curry, garlic, marjoram, mint, onion, oregano, parsley, black pepper, white pepper, rosemary, sesame seeds, thyme, turmeric.

Liver	Basil, chives, onion, oregano, black pepper, white pepper, sage.
Meatballs	Basil, celery, garlic, marjoram, onion, oregano, parsley, bell pepper, black pepper, rosemary, savory, thyme.
Pork*	Chili powder, cinnamon, cloves, garlic, onion, parsley, black pepper, cayenne pepper, white pepper, rosemary, sage, thyme.
Pot roast	Garlic, onion, parsley, black pepper, white pepper, thyme.
Turkey	Celery, onion, parsley, black pepper, white pepper, sage, thyme.
Veal*	Basil, curry powder, dill, lemon juice, onion, oregano, parsley, black pepper, white pepper, rosemary, sage, tarragon, thyme.

*Lean and trimmed meats.

Seafood	*Spices, Herbs, and Seasonings*
Fish	Basil, bay leaf, celery, chives, dill, fennel, ginger, lemon juice, mace, marjoram, onion, oregano, paprika, parsley, bell pepper, black pepper, rosemary, sage, sesame seeds, tarragon, thyme, turmeric.
Lobster	Garlic, lemon juice, onion, parsley, black pepper, tarragon, thyme.
Shrimp	Basil, bay leaf, celery, chives, dill, garlic, ginger, lemon juice, onion, oregano, parsley, bell pepper, black pepper, cayenne pepper, Tabasco.

Vegetables	*Spices, Herbs, and Seasonings*
Asparagus	Basil, bay leaf, lemon juice, parsley, tarragon, thyme.
Dried beans	Bay leaf, celery, garlic, mustard, onion, parsley, black pepper,

cayenne pepper, Tabasco, thyme.

Green beans   Basil, celery, garlic, onion, parsley, black pepper, sage, savory.

Lima beans   Bay leaf, celery, garlic, onion, parsley, black pepper, sage, savory.

Broccoli   Basil, caraway, curry powder, lemon juice, oregano, thyme.

Brussels sprouts   Marjoram, poppy seeds, rosemary, sage.

Cabbage   Caraway, celery, celery seeds, dill, mint, onion, parsley, black pepper, white pepper, Tabasco, tarragon.

Cauliflower   Cumin, curry powder, dill, marjoram, nutmeg, savory.

Eggplant   Celery, curry powder, dill, garlic, onion, oregano, parsley, black pepper, white pepper, rosemary, thyme.

Mushrooms	Marjoram, oregano, black pepper, rosemary, tarragon, thyme.
Onions	Basil, chives, garlic, oregano, black pepper, rosemary, sage, savory, thyme.
Peas	Basil, chives, garlic, onion, oregano, parsley, black pepper, rosemary, sage, savory, tarragon, thyme.
Spinach	Basil, chervil, garlic, marjoram, nutmeg, onion, parsley, black pepper, rosemary.
Squash	Basil, dill, garlic, onion, parsley, black pepper, white pepper, tarragon, thyme.
Sweet potatoes	Allspice, cinnamon, cloves, ginger, nutmeg, onion, thyme.
Tomatoes	Basil, chives, cloves, mace, marjoram, nutmeg, onion, oregano, parsley, black pepper, rosemary, tarragon.

Using Spices, Herbs, and Seasonings

Zucchini   Basil, dill, garlic, onion, parsley, black pepper, white pepper, tarragon, thyme.

Fruits	*Spices, Herbs, and Seasonings*
Most fruits	Cinnamon, cloves, ginger, mint, nutmeg, rosemary.

Dairy Products	*Spices, Herbs, and Seasonings*
Cheese	Chili powder, chives, mustard seed, paprika.
Eggs	Basil, chervil, chives, garlic, marjoram, nutmeg, onion, oregano, paprika, parsley, black pepper, cayenne pepper, rosemary, sage, Tabasco, tarragon, thyme, turmeric, Worcestershire sauce.

Whole Grains	*Spices, Herbs, and Seasonings*
Pasta and couscous	Basil, chives, cumin, fennel, marjoram, oregano, parsley, saffron.

Salads	*Spices, Herbs, and Seasonings*
Garden greens, with and without vegetables	Basil, chervil, chives, dill, garlic, marjoram, mint, onion, oregano, parsley, black pepper, tarragon, thyme.

Sauces	*Spices, Herbs, and Seasonings*
Cheese	Chives, curry powder, mustard, onion, paprika, parsley, cayenne pepper, Tabasco, Worcestershire sauce.
Creamy	Basil, chives, curry powder, horseradish, marjoram, onion, parsley, black pepper, cayenne pepper, Tabasco, tarragon, thyme, Worcestershire sauce.
Tomato	Basil, bay leaf, chervil, chives, fennel, garlic, onion, oregano, paprika, parsley, black pepper, cayenne pepper, sage, Tabasco, tarragon, thyme.

Soups	*Spices, Herbs, and Seasonings*
Bean	Basil, bay leaf, celery, chili powder, chives, garlic, onion, oregano, parsley, black pepper, cayenne pepper, rosemary, savory, Tabasco, thyme.
Chicken	Bay leaf, celery, chervil, chives, garlic, marjoram, onion, paprika, parsley, black pepper, cayenne pepper, sage, thyme.
Clear broth	Basil, paprika, parsley, black pepper.
Creamy broth	Bay leaf, celery, chives, lemon juice, parsley, black pepper.
Fish	Bay leaf, celery, chives, lemon juice, onion, parsley, bell pepper, black pepper, cayenne pepper, saffron, Tabasco, tarragon, thyme.
Gumbo	Basil, bay leaf, celery, filé, cumin, garlic, marjoram, parsley, black pepper, cayenne pepper, rosemary,

savory, Tabasco, thyme,
Worcestershire sauce.

Mushroom   Chives, garlic, parsley, black
pepper, cayenne pepper, tarragon.

Tomato   Allspice, basil, bay leaf, celery,
chives, garlic, onion, parsley, black
pepper, sage, tarragon, thyme.

Vegetable   Allspice, basil, bay leaf, celery,
chives, marjoram, onion, parsley,
black pepper, Tabasco, tarragon,
Worcestershire sauce.

Table 5: Characteristics and Uses of Various Spices, Herbs, and Seasonings

Spices, Herbs, or Seasonings	*Characteristics and Uses*
Allspice	Aroma is similar to a mixture of clove, cinnamon, and nutmeg. Good with fish, meats, beans and most vegetables, tomatoes, and gravies.

Anise	Flavor of licorice. Good with breads, fish, and meats.
Basil	Sweet warm flavor with an aromatic odor. Good with eggs, meats, tomatoes, gravies, beans, and dressings.
Bay leaves	Pungent flavor. Good with meats, seafood, asparagus, artichokes, tomatoes, beans, soups, gumbos, dressings, and tomato sauces.
Caraway seed	Spicy smell and aromatic taste. Good with meats, coleslaw, cabbage dishes, and rye breads.
Cardamom	Good with curries, breads, and soups.
Celery seed	Flavor of celery. Good with fish, beef, vegetables, soups, and salads.
Chervil	Mild and delicate flavor. Good with eggs, chicken, peas, spinach, and green salads.

Chili powder	Moderate to very hot flavor. Good with meats, eggs, beans, sauces, and gravies.
Chives	Sweet mild flavor of onion. Good with fish, salads, and soups.
Cinnamon	Good with custards, puddings, fruits, and oatmeal.
Cloves	From a pungent tropical tree with a distinctive flavor. Good with baked meats, fruits, beans, juices, onions, sweet potatoes, and tomatoes.
Coriander	A main ingredient in chili powder and curry powder. Good with baked meats, lamb, stuffings, soups, stews, gumbos, and sausage.
Curry powder	Distinctive and strong flavor. Good with meats, rice, chicken, lamb, fish, and vegetables.
Dill	Sharp taste. Good with cauliflower, cucumber, cabbage and other

Using Spices, Herbs, and Seasonings

vegetables, sauces, salads, stews, soups, fish, and meats.

Fennel	Stimulates the appetite. So good on hors d'oeuvres. Sweet hot flavor. Good with fish, soups, sauces, and breads.
Filé	Ground sassafras leaves. Good with gumbo.
Ginger	A pungent root. Essential in oriental cooking. Good with beverages, baked products, soups, meat dishes, and sauces.
Horseradish	Extremely aromatic. Good with sauces, roast beef, and oily fish.
Mace	Similar to nutmeg with a fragrant, delicate difference. Good with fish, tomatoes, and baked products.
Marjoram	Minty-sweet flavor. Good with meats, chicken, lamb, fish,

vegetables, dressings, soups, and stews.

Mint	Aromatic with a cool flavor. Good with meats especially lamb, sauces, peas, and ice tea.
Mustard	Pungent flavor. Good with meats, sauces, beans, salads, and dressings.
Nutmeg	Aromatic with slightly bitter flavor. Good with chicken, sweet potatoes, spinach, eggnog, toasted cheese, and cauliflower.
Oregano	Strong aromatic odor with slightly bitter flavor. Good with tomato sauces, fish, eggs, chicken, stews, gravies, soups, and vegetables.
Paprika	Pleasant odor with mild sweet flavor. Good with meats, fish, eggs, stews, soups, vegetables, and salad dressings.

Parsley	Mild, slightly tangy flavor. Good with meats, vegetables, soups, sauces, gravies, and as a condiment to freshen your breath.
Pepper, black	Pungent flavor. Good with all meats, particularly chicken and turkey, gravies, and vegetables.
Pepper, cayenne	Adds a pungent, hot chili pepper taste. Good with meats, eggs, sauces, and dried bean recipes.
Pepper, white	Ground after the peppercorn skin has been removed. Good with meats, gravies, and vegetables.
Peppercorns	The dried, unripe pepperberry. Good with meats and soups.
Poppy seeds	Rich fragrance with crunchy, nutlike flavor. Good with breads.
Rosemary	Aromatic with slightly piney taste. Good with fish, meats,

lamb, chicken, eggs, sauces, gravies, soups, and vegetables.

Saffron   Pungent and warmly aromatic. Good with baked meats, chicken, rice, and fish soups.

Sage   Camphoraceous and minty flavor. Good with sausage, meatloaf, hamburger, fish, pork, eggs, stuffing, stews, soups, sauces, gravies, and vegetables.

Salt   Flavor all its own. Good with meats, chicken, fish, gravies, sauces, dressings, soups, and eggs. Use sparingly in preparing food and try to avoid additional salt at the table.

Savory   Closely related to mint. Good with meats, especially chicken, sauces, gravies, soups, stews, salads, and dressings.

Sesame seeds	Seeds have a nutty, aromatic taste. Good with breads, fish, chicken, and lamb.
Stevia	Herbal sweetener—sugar substitute, but beware if mixed with maltodextrin (especially if diabetic).
Tabasco sauce	Very hot sauce. Good with meats, seafood, sauces, soups, gumbos, and eggs.
Tarragon	Pungent hot taste. Good with meats, chicken, sauces, tomatoes, salads, and dressings.
Thyme	Strong distinctive flavor. Good with meats, fish, chicken, soups, sauces, gravies, stuffing, stews, gumbo, and vegetables.
Turmeric	Mild ginger-pepper flavor. Good with eggs, meats, lamb, chicken, fish, eggs, salads, and dressings.

| Vanilla | From cured seedpod of the vanilla vine, a member of the orchid family. Enhances ice creams, custards, and stewed fruits. |

IV | Breakfast

Get the day going right with a hearty breakfast. This does not mean having a high-protein ham and egg breakfast every day, or conversely, having a bowl of oatmeal every day. Both types of breakfast can be healthy and fit the SUGAR BUSTERS! lifestyle. The obvious benefit of a ham, egg, and a single slice of whole-grain toast breakfast is that it will maximize the rate of weight loss (other than starvation) you can achieve. On the other hand, eating large amounts of saturated fat contained in many ham, bacon, or sausage products every day can put you at higher risk of developing cardiovascular disease. Also, those with genetic tendencies toward high cholesterol should probably reduce foods containing high levels of dietary cholesterol.

Eating oatmeal every day, while a great way to get a good serving of carbohydrate to get the day started, may make it difficult for those with a somewhat lower metabolism to lose weight at an acceptable rate. So, enjoy your breakfasts and vary your choices from time to time. Also, skew your choices in the direction in which your particular needs demand; more protein during your weight loss stage and more high-fiber carbohydrates during your weight maintenance stage.

Eat plenty of fruit. Do not let yourself get too busy to consume an ample amount of this food that was a staple for all of your ancestors who lived below the Arctic Circle. If you do not eat fruit at breakfast, eat it as a midmorning or midafternoon snack. Alternatively, eat a selection of fruits for breakfast from time to time. Eating a breakfast of only fruit is healthy and will certainly not cause you to gain weight.

SUGAR BUSTERS! Guide to Breakfast Planning

Good Breakfast Ideas
Whole fruit is best, fresh-squeezed juice is

Breakfast Foods to Avoid
Sugar-sweetened juice drinks

next best, and juice
made from concentrate
with no sugar added is
acceptable (much of
the fiber has been
filtered out)

Whole-grain or stone-ground whole-wheat toast	White toast
Stone-ground whole-wheat bagels	White bagels
Whole-grain crackers	Regular crackers
	Croissants and pastries
Spreadable fruit with no sugar added	Sugar-sweetened jams, jellies, and preserves
Omelets and egg dishes (made from eggs or nonfat liquid egg substitute)	
Trimmed ham (not sugar-cured), in moderation	Sugar-cured ham

Breakfast

Canadian bacon and lean bacon (not sugar-cured), in moderation	Fatty or sugar-cured bacon
High bran and whole-grain cereals with no sugar added or with less than 3 grams added sugar: All-Bran Extra Fiber, 100% Bran, Oat Bran, Shredded Wheat 'N Bran	Rice- and corn-based cereals and all cereals with more than 3 grams sugar per serving (including Rice Krispies, Total, Grape-Nuts, cornflakes, shredded wheat with white flour, regular puffed wheat, and regular puffed rice)
Whole, rolled, or steel-cut oats	Cream of Wheat; flavored instant hot cereals
Most fresh fruit (including apricots, grapefruit, cherries, dates, strawberries, blueberries, kiwis, apples, peaches, nectarines, tangerines,	Pineapples, raisins, ripe bananas

Breakfast

oranges, mangoes,
and grapes)

Frozen or canned fruit with no sugar added	Frozen fruit with sugar added, canned fruit in syrup
Plain or fruit-flavored low-fat or nonfat yogurt with no sugar added	Sugar-sweetened yogurt
Reduced-fat cottage cheese	Cottage cheese with pineapple

Breakfast

Breakfast Recipes

Bagel and Cream Cheese, page 62
Cereals, page 63
Cheese and Green Onion Omelet, page 64
Eggs Benedict, page 65
Eggs Sardou, page 67
Florentine (Spinach) Omelet, page 69
Fresh Fruit and Yogurt, page 71
Hearty Oatmeal, page 72
Tidbit Omelet, page 73
"Meatless" Egg Breakfast, page 75
Savory Spanish Omelet, page 77
Spicy Huevos (Eggs), page 79
Fabulous French Toast, page 81
Tasty Toast, page 83
Western Omelet, page 84

Bagel and Cream Cheese—Whole-grain bagels are coming soon!

1 stone-ground whole-wheat bagel, halved
2 tablespoons reduced-fat cream cheese

Toast the bagel to desired darkness. Top each bagel half with a tablespoon of the cream cheese.

Serves 1.

Note: This tasty breakfast combination is not a high-glycemic one, so you can enjoy it often with a clear conscience. Take the cream cheese out of the fridge a little ahead of time and toast or at least warm the bagel. Room temperature cream cheese spread on a warm bagel is much more flavorful than cold cream cheese atop a cold bagel.

Breakfast

Cereals

There are few breakfast cereals without significant amounts of the various refined sugars. These sugars are listed in the ingredient list on the packages and include sugar, brown sugar, raw sugar, sucrose, glucose, dextrose, maltose, corn syrup, high fructose corn syrup, honey, and molasses. Other common additives which do not have to be listed in the sugar column on the products' labels but which still cause a significant glycemic or blood sugar–elevating response are maltodextrin (which causes a very high response), malted barley, and some of the sugar alcohols like sorbitol, and maltitol.

While the following cereals still deliver a moderate glycemic response, they are currently believed to be the most acceptable of the lot.
Fiber One
Fiber Wise
Oatmeal (see recipe page 72)
Pearled Barley
Shredded Wheat 'N Bran

Note: If you can't find acceptable cereals in your supermarket, try a natural or health foods store.

Cheese and Green Onion Omelet—A can't miss basic!

2 teaspoons olive or canola oil
2 green onions, trimmed and chopped, plus
    about 2 inches of green tops, chopped
⅛ teaspoon Lawry's or other seasoned salt
2 large eggs
Ground black pepper to taste
¼ cup grated mild cheddar cheese

Combine the oil, green onions, and seasoned salt in a small nonstick skillet. Cook over medium heat until the onions have softened, about 3 minutes. In a bowl, beat the eggs with the black pepper. Add the mixture to the skillet and stir briefly to lightly scramble the eggs. Without stirring, continue to cook until the eggs are softly set, about 2 minutes. Sprinkle the cheese on top. Tilt the pan away from you and, using a spatula, fold half of the omelet over to enclose the filling. Cook for 1 minute more to melt the cheese. Slide the omelet onto a plate and serve.

Serves 1.

Note: You can't miss with this basic all-time favorite. We use Lawry's salt in this recipe, but substitute any seasoned salt of your preference. You can also vary the formula by using sharp cheddar cheese for a little more kick.

Eggs Benedict—World renowned dish, and for a reason!

4 cups water

2 tablespoons white vinegar

2 large eggs

2 slices whole-grain bread

2 slices Canadian bacon, or ham slices trimmed and cut into 3-inch circles

3 tablespoons hollandaise sauce (see page 317 and 318)

Bring the water and vinegar to a simmer in a 2-quart saucepan. Crack each egg into a small bowl, slide into the water, and cook at a bare simmer for about 4 minutes, until the eggs are set. While the eggs poach, toast the bread and cut each slice into a 3-inch circle. Warm the Canadian bacon or ham for about 1 minute per side in a nonstick skillet. On each toast round, layer a slice of bacon or ham, and a poached egg. Drizzle each with 1½ tablespoons hollandaise sauce. Serve immediately.

Serves 1 or 2.

Note: This healthy rendition substitutes whole-grain toast for the typical English muffins, which have a considerably higher glycemic index. If you use ham instead of Canadian bacon, be sure to buy a variety that has not been sugar-cured. Homemade hollandaise sauce is the best (try one of the recipes on pages 317 and 318), but using commercial hollandaise makes this elegant breakfast very quick to prepare. For variety, you could also top the dish with warmed salsa or even drizzle with a little steak sauce, such as A.1. or Heinz.

Breakfast

Eggs Sardou—For artichoke lovers and no bread to boot!

4 cups water

2 tablespoons white vinegar

4 large eggs

4 canned artichoke bottoms, drained (or 4 artichoke hearts, drained and halved)

½ tablespoon butter

One 10-ounce package frozen creamed spinach, cooked according to package directions

¼ cup plus 2 tablespoons hollandaise sauce (see pages 317 and 318)

Salt and ground black pepper to taste

Bring the water and vinegar to a simmer in a 2-quart saucepan. Crack each egg into a small bowl, slide into the water, and cook at a bare simmer for about 4 minutes, until the eggs are set. Meanwhile, combine the artichoke bottoms and butter in a small skillet and warm over medium-low heat. Reheat the creamed spinach, if necessary. Spoon creamed spinach into 4 mounds and top each with an artichoke bottom. Set a poached egg in each artichoke bottom. Drizzle hollandaise sauce over each egg. Add salt and pepper to taste and serve.

Serves 2 or 4.

Note: No bread in this one, since the eggs are served atop artichoke bottoms. Fresh artichoke can be quite tender, but since it takes up to 45 minutes to steam and prepare, canned bottoms are suggested. (Use canned artichoke hearts if canned artichoke bottoms are not readily available in your area.) A rich New Orleans invention, this dish is usually served with creamed spinach and hollandaise sauce. If you prefer a slightly less filling rendition, omit the hollandaise.

Breakfast

Florentine (Spinach) Omelet—Almost anything with spinach is nutritious.

1 teaspoon butter

⅓ cup chopped yellow onion

3 large eggs

Salt and ground black pepper to taste

2 tablespoons Dijon mustard

1 cup cooked fresh or frozen spinach, well
  drained and squeezed dry

2 tablespoons grated Parmesan cheese

Combine the butter and onion in a medium nonstick skillet. Stirring constantly, cook over medium heat until the onion has softened, 3 to 4 minutes. In a bowl, beat the eggs with the salt, pepper, and mustard. Add the egg mixture to the skillet and stir briefly to lightly scramble. Without stirring, continue to cook until the eggs are softly set, about 2 minutes. Scatter the spinach over the eggs and sprinkle with the Parmesan cheese. Cover the pan and cook for 1 minute to heat through. Uncover, tilt the pan away from you, and fold half of the omelet over with a spatula to enclose the filling. Cook for an additional 30 seconds before sliding the omelet onto a plate. Cut it in half before serving.

Serves 2.

Note: Eggs are an excellent and inexpensive protein source. In addition, the spinach provides
significant amounts of the recommended daily
allowance of vitamin A, vitamin C, and folate,
as well as the minerals calcium and magnesium. If you prefer to use frozen spinach, know
that a 10-ounce package will yield 1 cup cooked.

Breakfast

Fresh Fruit and Yogurt—A sweet way to start the day!

½ cup plain low-fat or nonfat yogurt (no sugar added)
1½ cups any combination of 3 fresh fruits (such as apricot, kiwi, and nectarine), cubed if large
¼ small lemon or lime
4 whole-grain crackers
1 ounce Philadelphia Light or other reduced-fat cream cheese

Combine the yogurt and fruit in a bowl. Squeeze the lemon or lime over the mixture and stir well to blend. Spoon into 2 serving bowls and accompany with crackers spread with cream cheese.

Serves 2.

Note: For a quick but nutritious breakfast, prepare and mix the fruit the evening before and store overnight in the refrigerator. As long as you avoid such high-glycemic choices as banana, raisins, and pineapple, your options are unlimited—try different combinations of apple, berries, cherries, grapes, melon, orange, peach, plum, and tangerine.

Hearty Oatmeal—But no brown sugar please!

2 cups water
Pinch of salt
1 cup whole, rolled, or steel-cut oatmeal
Up to 3 packets artificial sweetener or 5
   teaspoons fructose powder
Milk or cream to taste (optional)

Combine the water and salt in a 1- to 1½-quart saucepan and bring to a boil over high heat. Slowly sprinkle in the oatmeal. Reduce the heat to medium-low and cook, stirring gently, for about 5 minutes, until thickened. Remove the pan from heat and let sit for 2 minutes before serving. Sweeten, if desired, and add milk or cream.

Serves 2.

Note: Oatmeal provides a natural and nutritious serving of carbohydrates that contains a significant amount of soluble fiber, but take care not to overcook, which would raise its glycemic index. The oatmeal is moist and creamy so the addition of a little milk (or cream, if you want to indulge yourself) is optional.

Breakfast

Tidbit Omelet—Don't throw away that spicy beef, lamb, or chicken!

¼ cup cubed leftover cooked beef, chicken,
   lamb, pork, or shrimp
2 large eggs
About 2 teaspoons chopped fresh herbs of your
   choice (see note below)
Salt and ground black pepper to taste

Put the leftover meat or shrimp in a small non-stick skillet. Cook over medium heat until thoroughly warmed through, 2 to 3 minutes. In a bowl, beat the eggs with the herbs, salt, and pepper. Add the egg mixture to the skillet and stir briefly to lightly scramble. Cook without stirring for about 2 minutes more, until the eggs are softly set. Tilt the skillet away from you. With a spatula, fold half of the omelet over to enclose the filling. Cook for 30 seconds more, then slide the omelet onto a plate and serve.

Serves 1.

Note: Man's best friend may have to do without now that you have this quick and easy recipe. The lesson is not to throw away that leftover meat or shrimp—save it for this easy and economical breakfast dish. Choose appropriate, and preferably fresh, seasoning for the type of meat or the shrimp you are using from the lists on pages 38–41. If the leftovers are highly seasoned to begin with, however, you may not need to add any more. Serve with a slice of whole-grain toast.

"Meatless" Egg Breakfast with Grilled Tomatoes—Eggs without the additional saturated fat.

1 tablespoon olive or canola oil
Three ¼-inch-thick slices tomato
Salt and ground black pepper to taste
1 or 2 large eggs
Fresh parsley sprigs, to garnish

Pour the oil into a small or medium (depending upon how many eggs you are cooking) nonstick grill pan. Warm over medium heat. When the oil is hot, add the tomato slices and cook until browned, about 1 minute per side, seasoning to taste with salt and pepper. Remove the tomatoes to a plate and add the egg(s) to the remaining oil in the pan. Cook for 2 to 3 minutes, until the white is set and the yellow is as set as desired. Add to the plate with the tomatoes, garnish with parsley sprigs, and serve immediately.

Serves 1.

Note: This is obviously not a meatless breakfast since it includes eggs, but we've added no extra saturated fat in the way of an accompanying meat. Many people eat too much bacon, ham, or sausage that has been sugar-cured and also contains a large amount of the limited daily allowance of saturated fat. Enjoy your eggs with 2 slices Tasty Toast (page 83).

Savory Spanish Omelet—Viva la Mexico!

¼ cup chopped yellow onion

1 small clove garlic, minced

2 tablespoons thinly sliced celery

½ cup chopped fresh tomato

1 tablespoon butter

2 tablespoons canned diced green chilies

3 large eggs

2 tablespoons water

¼ teaspoon salt

⅛ teaspoon ground black pepper

Tabasco or other hot sauce or salsa to taste (optional)

Combine the onion, garlic, celery, tomato, and ½ tablespoon of the butter in a large nonstick skillet. Cook over medium heat until the vegetables soften and the juices nearly evaporate, 7 to 8 minutes. Add the chilies and cook for 1 minute more. Meanwhile, beat the eggs with the water, salt, and black pepper in a small bowl. Remove the vegetables from the skillet and set them aside, adding the remaining ½ tablespoon butter to the pan. When it has melted, add the egg mixture and cook until the eggs are softly set, about 3 minutes. Scatter the cooked vegetables on top, tilt the pan away from you, and fold half of the omelet over with a spatula to enclose the filling. Cook for 30 seconds more to heat through. Slide the omelet onto a plate, cut it in half, and finish with a few dashes of hot sauce or a dollop of your favorite salsa, if desired. Serve immediately.

Serves 2.

Note: Omelets are among the most versatile of dishes. They can be made in minutes with any of dozens of filling variations—limited only by whim and what's on the pantry shelf. A few trial runs and you should have omelet-making techniques sufficiently mastered to make omelets a staple in your low-glycemic kitchen. And remember—if you mess up an omelet, the worst you will have is an equally tasty heap of scrambled eggs!

Spicy Huevos (Eggs) with Salsa—Green chilies and salsa are good on almost anything!

One 4-ounce can whole green chilies, drained
1 tablespoon butter
4 large eggs
Salt to taste
½ cup salsa

Cut the chilies into ½-inch-thick strips and arrange them to form a circle or square on each of 2 plates. For over-easy eggs, preheat a medium nonstick skillet over medium heat. Add the butter and heat until it sizzles. Crack each egg into the pan and add salt to taste. Reduce the heat to medium-low, and cook until the whites are firm and beginning to brown lightly on the bottom, about 2 minutes. Flip the eggs over and cook for another 10 to 15 seconds, until firm on the other side. For sunny-side up eggs, cover the pan when you reduce the heat and cook only on one side, until the whites are solid and the yolks are as runny or as hard as you like, 2½ to 3 minutes. Meanwhile, warm the salsa in a small microwave-safe dish in a microwave oven at full power for 1 to 2 minutes. Put a cooked egg in the center of each green chili frame and drizzle with 2 tablespoons warm salsa.

Serves 2.

Note: Cook the eggs to your liking—over-easy or sunny-side up. Make your own fresh salsa (see page 324) or use a favorite prepared variety. Old El Paso and Casa Fiesta are among the available brands of whole peeled green chilies. A slice or two of stone-ground whole-wheat bread makes a good accompaniment.

Breakfast

Fabulous French Toast—No syrup necessary!

1 large egg
$^1/_3$ cup milk
1 teaspoon Mexican Vanilla (accept no
   substitutions)
1 teaspoon ground cinnamon
1 teaspoon grated nutmeg (do this with fresh
   nutmeg, use a grater)
Sugar substitute to taste
2 tablespoons vegetable oil
2 slices SUGAR BUSTERS! stone-ground,
   whole-wheat bread (Rustic Loaf) or any whole-
   grain bread

In a shallow bowl, beat the egg. Add milk, vanilla, cinnamon, nutmeg, and sugar substitute and mix well. Add the bread and soak for about 5 minutes. Turn the bread over and continue to soak for a few minutes more, until all the egg mixture has been absorbed. Heat the oil in a medium skillet over medium heat. Add the bread and cook until well browned, 1 to 2 minutes per side. Serve with dusted cinnamon and add a bit more sugar substitute if desired.

Serves 1.

Note: This is a favorite recipe of Sheila Leach of New Orleans who lost over 80 pounds following the SUGAR BUSTERS! lifestyle. See her before and after pictures on the next page.

Sheila Leach, before SUGAR BUSTERS!

Sheila Leach, after.

Tasty Toast—Once you have ceased eating refined sugar, this toast tastes like cake!

2 tablespoons olive oil
2 slices stone-ground whole-wheat bread

Pour the oil into a medium nonstick skillet over medium heat. Add the bread to the skillet, quickly turning to coat the slices on both sides with the oil. Cook until the toast is well browned, about 1 minute per side, taking care not to let it burn.

Serves 1.

Note: Enjoy it with coffee, tea, or low-fat milk. For a little extra flavor, add two strips of any citrus peel to the pan (lemon, orange, or lime) while you are heating the oil.

Western Omelet—A cowboy's delight!

3 tablespoons chopped yellow onion

2 tablespoons finely chopped red and/or green
  bell pepper

⅓ cup thinly sliced white button mushrooms

¼ cup diced ham (not sugar-cured)

2 teaspoons canola oil

4 large eggs

Salt and ground black pepper to taste

⅓ cup grated sharp cheddar cheese

Preheat a broiler. Combine the onion, bell pepper, mushrooms, ham, and oil in a medium nonstick skillet with an ovenproof handle. Stirring constantly, cook over medium heat until the vegetables have softened, 4 to 5 minutes. Beat the eggs with the salt and black pepper in a bowl and add them to the skillet. Cook until the eggs are softly set, about 3 minutes. Sprinkle the cheese on top, transfer the skillet to the broiler, and broil until puffed and golden, 1 to 2 minutes. With a spatula, cut the omelet in half and carefully lift each half out of the pan. Serve piping hot.

Serves 2.

Note: This hearty "ranchman" breakfast provides a good combination of protein and carbohydrates and should keep you quite satisfied until your midmorning snack of a nice piece of fruit or a few nuts. It's so big it would be difficult to flip, so we just stick it under the broiler and let it puff up instead. Serve with stone-ground whole-wheat toast.

V | Lunch

This is the meal least likely to be prepared at home during the week. But weekends do come, and often the clock strikes noon or the stomach growls right in the middle of your catch-up projects. These particular recipes are presented to allow you to have a minimum amount of interruption to your midweek or weekend work or play. We want these recipes to be quick and easy but certainly not bland. If you like a bland lunch, reduce the amount of the ingredients that you think are making the dishes spicier than your palates. Conversely, crank up such spices if that really turns you on!

One significant advantage of a low-glycemic lunch is that you will not ultimately be subjected to the same level of low-sugar (hypoglycemic) response that you would get if you ate a sugar filled, high-glycemic lunch. A high glycemic lunch for many of you would drive up your blood sugar which would soon be followed (within one hour or less) by a rapid fall in blood sugar, making you either lethargic, sleepy, have sweaty palms, nervous, or irritable. Wouldn't it be nice to eat a full-size lunch and not have to put up with such consequences?

Please remember, for the lunch recipes, and dinner, too, anytime you see the requirement for a can of this or that, we would prefer that you use the fresh version and then the frozen version to yield the best possible gastronomic and glycemic results. Canned portions simply represent the quickest and easiest way to get something on the table. Enjoy your lunch!

SUGAR BUSTERS! Guide to Lunch Planning

Good Lunch Ideas
Milk, juices with no sugar added, iced tea with no sugar added, artificially sweetened lemonade, diet colas—

Lunch Foods to Avoid
Sugar-sweetened juices, iced tea, lemonade, and colas

all liquids in
moderation at
meal-time, even water

Stone-ground (coarse) semolina pasta dishes	White flour pasta dishes
Brown rice or brown basmati rice, in moderation	White rice
Trimmed lean meats and skinned poultry All nonbreaded seafood	Fatty meats and poultry skin, cold cuts with sugar added
Broiled tomatoes, mushrooms, beans and lentils, sweet potatoes, in moderation	French fries, baked and other white and red potatoes, corn
Most fresh, frozen, and canned vegetables	Beets, carrots, parsnips, turnips, and frozen or canned vegetables with sugar added

Lunch

Whole-grain and stone-ground whole-wheat breads, pumpernickel	White bread, French bread, Italian bread
Stone-ground pitas	Regular pitas
Stone-ground whole-wheat tortillas	Corn and white flour tortillas
Whole-grain crackers	Regular crackers Rice cakes
Natural peanut butter with no sugar added	Peanut butter with sugar added
Spreadable fruit with no sugar added	Sugar-sweetened jams, jellies, and preserves
Homemade soups and commercial soups with no sugar or white flour added	Corn- and potato-based soups, rice soups, soups with sugar or white flour added
Nuts, dill pickles	Chips, pretzels, sweet pickles

Lunch

Most fresh fruit (including apricots, grapefruit, cherries, strawberries, blueberries, kiwis, apples, peaches, nectarines, tangerines, oranges, mangoes, and grapes)	Pineapples, raisins, ripe bananas, watermelons
Naturally sweetened frozen or canned fruit with no sugar added	Frozen fruit with sugar added, canned fruit in syrup
Plain or fruit-flavored low-fat or nonfat yogurt with no sugar added	Sugar-sweetened yogurt
Reduced-fat cottage cheese	Cottage cheese with pineapple
Nuts, cheese, sugar-free ice cream	Cookies, cake, regular ice cream

Lunch Recipes

Chicken Mexicano, page 93

Chicken Caesar Salad, page 94

Stir-Fried Ginger Chicken, page 95

Tarragon Chicken Salad, page 97

Crab Cakes, page 98

Crab Salad, page 100

Egg Salad in Tomato Shells, page 101

Fish Fillets and Skillet Vegetables, page 103

Green Chilies Cheese Casserole, page 105

Guacamole Salad, page 106

Chilled Lentil Salad, page 108

Lawry Burgers, page 109

Whole-Wheat Spaghetti with
   Olive-Tomato Sauce, page 110

Fettucine with "Raw"
   Tomato Sauce, page 112

Fourth of July Macaroni Salad, page 113

Seared Shrimp Salad, page 114

Bayou Spicy Boiled Shrimp, page 115

Shrimp and Scallop "Goulash", page 116

Shrimp Salad, page 118

Fresh Spinach Salad with Bacon, page 119

Classic Tuna Salad, page 120

Blackened Tuna Salad, page 121

Lunch

Soups

Italian Artichoke Soup, page 123

No-Cook Chunky Avocado Soup, page 125

Quick-Draw Black Bean Soup, page 127

Traditional Black Bean Soup, page 129

Garlic–White Bean Soup, page 131

Chicken Soup with Tomatoes
    and Green Beans, page, 133

Simple Chicken Soup, page 135

French Onion Soup, page 136

Gazpacho Soup, page 138

Green Chili and Jalapeño Soup, page 140

Sweet Potato Soup, page 142

Cool Tomato and Cucumber Soup, page 144

Tortillaless Soup, page 146

Lunch

Chicken Mexicano—Viva Zapata!

2⅔ cups shredded cooked chicken
One 4-ounce can chopped green chilies
2 tablespoons canned sliced jalapeño peppers
2 cups grated longhorn or Monterey Jack cheese
One 10-ounce can enchilada sauce
One 10¾-ounce can cream of chicken soup
½ cup evaporated milk
½ cup low-fat milk
3 cups cooked brown rice
Chopped fresh cilantro, to garnish

Preheat the oven to 350 degrees. Combine the chicken, green chilies, jalapeño peppers, and cheese in an ovenproof 2-quart glass casserole. Add the enchilada sauce, soup, evaporated milk, and milk. Mix well. Bake for about 20 minutes, until hot and bubbly. Put ½ cup brown rice in each of 6 large, shallow bowls, ladle 1 cup of the chicken casserole on top, and garnish with a sprinkling of cilantro.

Serves 6.

Note: This easy one-dish lunch is rich and robustly flavorful. It's an admitted indulgence, a bit high in fat and calories, so make it only on occasion.

Chicken Caesar Salad—A true classic.

One 10-ounce package cut up romaine lettuce
⅔ cup Caesar Dressing (see page 307)
1-2 cups cooked shredded chicken breast or the
    equivalent of 1-2 large chicken breasts
1 cup whole-wheat croutons
2 tablespoons shredded Parmesan cheese

In a large bowl, combine the lettuce and Caesar
Dressing. Toss to coat and divide among 4 salad
plates. Lay slices of chicken over each. Scatter
croutons and Parmesan cheese on top.

Serves 4.

Note: Once a fancy restaurant exclusive, Caesar
salad is now an everyday meal—it's healthy, filling, and ever so versatile. This rendition is
topped with slivers of tasty, tender chicken
breast meat. Be sure to use whole-wheat croutons; you can make your own from slices of
stone-ground whole-wheat toast. The salad is
best with shredded rather than grated Parmesan
cheese.

Stir-Fried Ginger Chicken—
A low-glycemic dish.

2 tablespoons olive, canola, or peanut oil

1 medium yellow onion, sliced

1 teaspoon garlic salt

1 medium red bell pepper, cored, seeded, and
  cut into thin strips

1 tablespoon coarsely grated fresh ginger

2 cups cooked shredded chicken breast or the
  equivalent of 2 large chicken breasts

1 medium tomato, cut into thin wedges

2 tablespoons balsamic vinegar

Preheat a nonstick stir-fry pan or a large nonstick skillet over high heat. Add the oil, onion,
and garlic salt and stir-fry until the onion turns
translucent, about 1½ minutes. Add the bell
pepper and ginger and stir-fry for 1 minute. Add
the chicken and tomato and stir-fry for about
2 minutes more, until the vegetables are soft.
Stir in the vinegar, stir-fry for 30 seconds more,
and serve.

Serves 2.

Note: One taste and this quick and easy, low-
glycemic meal will become a regular in your

kitchen. Stir-fries are healthy, simple, and fun and require only a few guidelines—get the pan hot before you start, cut the food into pieces of about the same size to promote even cooking, and keep it moving with a wooden spoon or paddle or two. This stir-fry gets a special accent from Italian balsamic vinegar, a once exotic import now stocked by most supermarkets.

Tarragon Chicken Salad—Let's eat some poultry!

1⅓ cups coarsely chopped cooked chicken
    breast
½ cup chopped celery
3 tablespoons mayonnaise
1 clove garlic, peeled
¼ teaspoon onion powder
¼ teaspoon dried tarragon

Combine the chicken, celery, and mayonnaise in a medium bowl. Mix well to coat. Press in the garlic, then mix in the onion powder and tarragon.

Serves 2.

Note: Simple and satisfying, a perfect summer-time treat. Serve it at room temperature or chilled, by itself, on a bed of lettuce, or in a stone-ground pita.

Chesapeake Crab Cakes—A great Northeast treat!

1 slice toasted stone-ground whole-wheat bread

1 pound fresh, frozen (thawed), or canned (drained) lump crabmeat, (cartilage and shell picked out)

2 large eggs, beaten

2 tablespoons sour cream

1 tablespoon Dijon mustard

¼ teaspoon hot sauce

¼ teaspoon ground black pepper

2 tablespoons olive oil

Break the toast up and pulse a few times in a food processor to make crumbs. Combine the crabmeat, eggs, sour cream, mustard, hot sauce, pepper, and bread crumbs in a large bowl and mix well. Using about ⅔ cup of the mixture for each, form 4 cakes. Cover and chill in the refrigerator for about 1 hour to firm. Preheat a large nonstick skillet over medium-high heat. Swirl in the oil, then add the crab cakes. Cook until firm and golden, about 6 minutes per side. Serve 2 cakes per person.

Serves 2.

Note: Everybody loves this Northeast regional specialty. Serve with lemon wedges and home-made salsa (see page 324) or prepared salsa. Pair the crab cakes with your favorite green salad or one of the slaws on pages 244 to 248. For an ap-petizer, form 8 little cakes using about ⅓ cup of the crab mixture for each, and cook them for only about 3 minutes per side.

Crab Salad—Best if made with Gulf of Mexico blue point crabs.

1 pound fresh lump crabmeat, cartilage and
   shell picked out
1 hard-boiled egg, chopped
2 tablespoons chopped yellow onion
2 tablespoons thinly sliced shallot (bulb only)
1½ tablespoons chopped celery
1½ tablespoons chopped dill pickle
2 tablespoons mayonnaise
¼ teaspoon French's yellow mustard
Salt and ground black pepper to taste
Heavy sprinkling of paprika, to garnish

In a large bowl, combine the crabmeat, egg, onion, shallot, celery, and pickle. Mix together the mayonnaise and mustard in a small bowl. Add the mixture to the crab and toss to coat. Salt and pepper to taste and garnish with paprika.

Serves 6.

Note: Party fare sure to please, this recipe can easily be made with a combination of shrimp and crabmeat. Serve the salad on a bed of lettuce.

Egg Salad in Tomato Shells—Two nutritious ingredients make a healthy dish.

4 medium tomatoes
One 3-ounce package reduced-fat cream cheese
2 tablespoons low-fat milk
¼ cup mayonnaise
3 hard-boiled eggs, chopped
¼ cup chopped green bell pepper
¼ cup peeled, seeded, and chopped cucumber
2 tablespoons chopped green onion
¼ teaspoon hot sauce (optional)
Salt to taste

To hollow out each tomato shell, first slice ¼ inch off the top. With a spoon, scoop out the inside pulp, taking care to remove the seeds and leaving intact the meat attached to the outer skin. Combine the cream cheese, milk, and mayonnaise in a medium bowl and blend thoroughly with a whisk. Add the eggs, bell pepper, cucumber, green onion, hot sauce, if desired, and salt. Chill in the freezer for 10 minutes. Spoon a generous ⅓ cup of the cold salad into each tomato shell. Serve with additional mayonnaise on the side, if desired.

Serves 4.

Note: Nutritious eggs and tomatoes team up to make this classic dish as good for you as it is good—and it tastes just as good now as when Mom made it. Chilling and firming the salad in the freezer is a lot faster than doing so in the refrigerator. For a bite-size hors d'oeuvre version, spoon the egg salad into 24 hollowed-out cherry tomatoes.

Fish Fillets and Skillet Vegetables—Healthy and tasty.

2 tablespoons olive oil
⅓ cup thinly sliced yellow onion
1 teaspoon dried oregano
1 medium zucchini, thinly sliced
1 medium tomato, cut into thin wedges
12 ounces white fish fillets (see note below)
1 teaspoon salt
½ teaspoon ground black pepper
¼ cup grated mozzarella cheese
¼ cup grated provolone cheese

Combine the oil and onions in a large skillet. Sprinkle with oregano and sauté over medium heat until the onions are translucent, about 2 minutes. Stir in the zucchini and cook for 2 minutes more. Add the tomato and stir. Lay the fish fillets on top of the vegetables. Sprinkle with salt and pepper. Reduce the heat to medium-low, cover, and simmer for about 8 minutes, until the fish flakes easily. Sprinkle the fish with the cheeses. Re-cover and cook until the cheese has melted, about 2 minutes. Transfer the fillets to dinner plates, and serve the vegetables on the side.

Serves 2.

Note: There's nothing plain about this "plain piece of fish," since we serve it up with a cheese topping and a skilletful of vegetables. Choose a nonoily fish, such as orange roughy or trout.

Lunch

Green Chilies Cheese Casserole—How simple can it get?

6 large eggs
4 cups grated sharp cheddar cheese
Two 4-ounce cans diced green chilies

Preheat the oven to 350 degrees. Crack the eggs into a large bowl and beat. Add the cheese and green chilies. Mix, pour into a 9-by-13-inch baking dish, and spread evenly across the dish. Bake for about 25 minutes, until the casserole has set and lightly browned. Cut into 6 squares and serve.

Serves 6.

Note: Just combine ingredients (the canned green chilies are already seeded and diced), and pop into the oven. This "Mexican quiche" will be ready to please in but 25 minutes. If you like things hot and spicy, add a dash of your favorite salsa.

Guacamole Salad—Now popular nationwide!

2 ripe avocados

2 teaspoons fresh lemon juice

¾ teaspoon salt

2 green onions trimmed and thinly sliced

4 cherry tomatoes, chopped (optional)

½ tablespoon finely chopped fresh cilantro
   (optional)

1 clove garlic, peeled

4 cups mixed salad greens

Cut the avocados in half, remove the pits, and scoop out the flesh with a spoon. Combine with the lemon juice and salt in a bowl and mash. Add the green onions, and, if desired, tomatoes and cilantro. Press in the garlic. Chill in the freezer for 10 minutes. Mound the greens on 2 large or 4 small salad plates, and top each with guacamole.

Serves 2 as a main course salad or 4 as a side salad.

Note: Once a regional delicacy, guacamole is now popular across the country. Don't worry too much about the considerable fat in avocados— it's primarily monounsaturated and polyunsaturated fat. Be sure to use ripe avocados. For a real treat, substitute the juice of key limes, the small, flavorful south Florida variety, for that of the lemon juice. If you like your guacamole salad spicy, serve it with a hot salsa or ½ teaspoon of seeded and chopped jalapeño pepper. To make about 1 pint of dip, omit the salad greens.

Chilled Lentil Salad—A very heart-healthy salad.

6 cups water
2 cups dried lentils, picked over
2 medium tomatoes, seeded and chopped
½ cup chopped celery
⅔ cup olive oil
⅓ cup fresh lemon juice
4 cloves garlic, minced
2 teaspoons Italian seasoning
½ teaspoon salt
¼ teaspoon ground black pepper

Lunch

Bring the water to a boil in a 3-quart saucepan. Add the lentils and boil for 15 minutes. Drain, remove the lentils to a mixing bowl, and chill for 15 minutes in the freezer. Add the tomatoes and celery. In another bowl, combine the oil, lemon juice, garlic, Italian seasoning, salt, and pepper for a dressing. Pour the dressing over the lentils and toss to coat.

Serves 6.

Note: Heart-healthy lentils are the star of this salad. Use brown, green, or red lentils, but take care not to overcook them—they should still have a bit of crunch when they hit the salad plate. Serve on lettuce leaves.

Lawry Burgers—A hamburger steak in disguise.

1 pound ground beef chuck
½ cup chopped yellow onion
2 tablespoons finely chopped fresh flat-leaf
   parsley
1 tablespoon Dijon mustard
1 teaspoon Worcestershire sauce
½ teaspoon ground black pepper
½ teaspoon Lawry's Seasoned Salt
Dash of hot sauce (or more, to taste)

In a large bowl, combine the meat, onion, parsley, mustard, Worcestershire sauce, pepper, seasoned salt, and hot sauce. Mix well and form into 4 patties. Place the patties in a large nonstick skillet, and cook over medium heat for 3 to 6 minutes per side, to desired doneness.

Serves 4.

Note: Eat these ¼-pounders, which get their distinctive flavor from the use of seasoned salt, without a bun but with your favorite burger accompaniments—ketchup, spicy mustard, pickle relish, and salsa. Cook the burgers to your liking—3 to 4 minutes per side will yield burgers that are medium-rare, 6 minutes well-done (but also dry!).

Lunch

Whole-Wheat Spaghetti with Olive-Tomato Sauce—A rural Italian staple.

¼ cup olive oil
1 medium yellow onion, chopped
6 large cloves garlic, chopped
⅓ cup dry white wine
One 28-ounce can diced tomatoes
½ cup chopped black olives
¼ cup chopped fresh basil
¼ teaspoon crushed red pepper flakes
½ pound whole-wheat spaghetti
2 tablespoons grated Parmesan cheese

Preheat a large nonstick skillet over medium heat. Add the oil and onion and cook, stirring constantly, until the onion is golden and soft, about 5 minutes. Stir in the garlic and continue to cook and stir until it gives off an aroma, about 30 seconds. Add the wine and cook for 1 minute. Stir in the tomatoes, olives, basil, and red pepper flakes. Cook until a thick sauce forms, 15 to 17 minutes. Meanwhile, bring a large pot of water (about 8 cups) to a boil. Stir in the pasta and cook to desired doneness, 8 to 9 minutes. Drain the pasta and return it to the pot. Add the sauce and the Parmesan cheese, and toss to coat.

Serves 4.

Note: This hearty pasta dish is topped with a simplified version of a traditional Italian olive and tomato sauce. Because the sauce is brimming with chunks of vegetables, you needn't use an inordinate quantity of pasta. Be sure to choose an organic whole-wheat pasta, not one that has been made from refined flour. Use whole-wheat fettucine if you prefer.

Fettucine with "Raw" Tomato Sauce—You only cook the fettucine.

½ pound whole-wheat fettucine (or spaghetti)

One 12-ounce carton cherry tomatoes, cut into eighths

2 green onions, trimmed and chopped

¼ cup chopped fresh basil

⅓ cup olive oil

2 tablespoons fresh lemon juice

½ teaspoon salt

¼ teaspoon ground black pepper

Bring a large pot of water (about 8 cups) to a boil. Stir in the pasta and cook to desired doneness, 8 to 9 minutes. While the pasta cooks, combine the tomatoes, green onion, basil, oil, lemon juice, salt, and pepper in a large bowl. Drain the pasta and add it to the bowl. Toss to coat and serve immediately.

Serves 4.

Note: You don't have to cook this fabulous and fast tomato sauce—the warmth of the pasta will "cook" it sufficiently when the pasta is tossed in it. This is a great entertaining recipe that can easily be doubled or tripled.

Fourth of July Macaroni Salad—What a way to celebrate!

¼ pound whole-wheat elbow macaroni
¼ cup chopped red onion
¼ cup chopped green bell pepper
1 medium tomato, roughly chopped
2 tablespoons sliced pimiento-stuffed green olives
¼ cup mayonnaise
1 tablespoon red wine vinegar
1 teaspoon Dijon mustard
¼ teaspoon salt
⅛ teaspoon ground black pepper

Bring a medium pot of water (about 4 cups) to a boil. Add the macaroni and cook until al dente, 7 to 8 minutes. Meanwhile, combine the onion, bell pepper, tomato, and olives in a large bowl. In a small bowl, mix together the mayonnaise, vinegar, mustard, salt, and black pepper. Drain and add the pasta to the bowl. Add the mayonnaise mixture and toss to coat. Chill thoroughly before serving.

Serves 4.

Note: Perfect for the backyard picnic, this salad is colorful and chock full of onion, bell pepper, and olives. You could easily add cooked chicken or shrimp for an even more substantial lunch.

Seared Shrimp Salad—Shrimp are good any way you cook them.

1 teaspoon garlic powder
½ to 1 tablespoon ground black pepper
½ teaspoon salt
⅛ teaspoon dried oregano
1 pound large shrimp, peeled and deveined
1 head romaine lettuce
½ cup Caesar Dressing (page 307)

Mix together the garlic powder, pepper, salt, and oregano in a medium bowl. Add the shrimp and toss to coat. Preheat a heavy nonstick skillet over high heat. Add the shrimp and sear until dark brown (almost burnt), 1 to 2 minutes per side. In a large bowl, combine the lettuce and the dressing and toss to mix thoroughly. Divide the salad among 4 plates and serve the shrimp on top.

Serves 4.

Note: If you ever run out of cooking oil, this is a dish you can prepare without having to make a quick trip to the grocery for more! The recipe is as versatile as it is easy—you could easily substitute chicken breasts, fish fillets, rib-eye steaks, or pork chops for the shrimp, increasing the cooking time to 4 to 5 minutes per side.

Bayou Spicy Boiled Shrimp—A Southern staple.

12 cups water
One 3-ounce bag Zatarain's Shrimp and Crab
  Boil or other seafood seasoning
1 tablespoon salt
½ teaspoon cayenne pepper (optional)
Juice of 2 lemons
4 pounds shrimp in the shells

Bring the water to a boil in a large pot. Add the seafood seasoning, salt, cayenne pepper, if desired, lemon juice, and shrimp. Bring back to a boil, cover, and boil for 10 minutes. Remove the pot from the heat and set aside for 15 minutes. Drain and serve.

Serves 4 for dinner, 12 as hors d'oeuvres.

Note: Use any size shrimp, and serve them any way you like—warm or chilled, peeled or not, plain or with some Remoulade Sauce (page 323). In New Orleans, we like to boil our shrimp with the heads on, but this variety is hard to find in many other parts of the country. If you do cook heads-on shrimp, increase the amount of salt used to 3 tablespoons and the amount of cayenne pepper, if you add it, to 1 teaspoon.

Shrimp and Scallop "Goulash"—An interesting combination.

2 cups water

1 pound small shrimp, peeled and deveined

1 pound scallops (whole bay scallops or
  quartered sea scallops)

½ head cauliflower, divided into florets

One 12-ounce basket cherry tomatoes, halved

¼ cup plus 2 tablespoons pitted black olives,
  quartered, or 3 tablespoons capers, drained

One 8-ounce can sliced water chestnuts,
  drained

Sauce:

2 cups mayonnaise

½ cup horseradish sauce

2 tablespoons dry mustard

1 teaspoon fresh lemon juice

½ teaspoon salt

½ teaspoon ground black pepper

Bring the water to a simmer in a 2-quart sauce-pan. Reduce the heat to low and add the shrimp. Cook for 1 minute. Add the scallops and cook for 1 minute more. Drain, transfer to a large bowl, and let cool. Meanwhile, combine all ingredients for the sauce in a small bowl. Add the cauliflower, tomatoes, olives or capers, and water chestnuts to the shrimp and scallop mixture. Add the sauce and toss to coat. Serve immediately or cover and chill in the refrigerator.

Serves 4 to 6.

Note: Paired with a green salad and whole-grain crackers, this makes a terrific warm weather lunch. The flavorful horseradish sauce gives the dressing its creamy texture; for added zest, stir in 1 tablespoon prepared horseradish. Use either tiny bay scallops (tasty, but not always available) or larger sea scallops that have been quartered.

Shrimp Salad—Particularly flavorful.

1 pound cooked, peeled small shrimp
1 hard-boiled egg, chopped
1½ tablespoons chopped celery
1½ tablespoons chopped dill pickle
2 tablespoons thinly sliced shallot (bulb only)
2 tablespoons chopped yellow onion
2 tablespoons mayonnaise
1 teaspoon French's yellow mustard
Salt and pepper to taste
Paprika, heavy sprinkling

In a large bowl, combine the shrimp, egg, celery, pickle, shallot, and onion. Mix together the mayonnaise and mustard in a small bowl. Add the mixture to the shrimp and toss to coat. Salt and pepper to taste and garnish with paprika.

Serves 6.

Note: Perfect and flavorful as is, the salad can also be made with ½ pound lump crabmeat, cartilage and shells picked out, in place of half of the shrimp for variety. The recipe can easily be doubled or tripled for a big get-together. Serve it on a bed of lettuce or mixed greens.

Fresh Spinach Salad with Bacon—Raw spinach is the most nutritious.

One 10-ounce package fresh salad spinach
3 strips crisp cooked bacon, crumbled
One 4-ounce can hearts of palm, drained and
    sliced
¼ teaspoon garlic salt
Scant ½ cup Cider Vinaigrette (page 314)
2 hard-boiled eggs, sliced

In a large bowl, mix together the spinach, bacon, hearts of palm, and garlic salt. Add the Cider Vinaigrette, toss to coat, and garnish with the sliced egg.

Serves 4.

Note: Raw is the most nutritious way to eat spinach—and one of the most delicious when served up in this satisfying main course salad. Look for spinach marked "salad," which has already been cleaned. Use turkey bacon if you're concerned about the fat in regular bacon. Hearts of palm, which are readily available canned, taste a bit like artichokes.

Classic Tuna Salad—A historic favorite for lunch.

Two 6-ounce cans white tuna packed in water,
   drained
1 hard-boiled egg, chopped
¼ cup chopped celery
¼ cup minced kosher dill pickle
¼ cup mayonnaise
1½ tablespoons fresh lemon juice
Salt and ground black pepper to taste

In a large bowl, combine the tuna, egg, celery, pickle, mayonnaise, lemon juice, salt, and pepper. Mix well.

Serves 3 to 4.

Note: For a historic luncheon favorite with a new twist, this tuna salad can be eaten rolled in a lettuce leaf. Tuna, a cold water fish, is a good source of omega-3 fatty acid. Select white tuna, preferably albacore.

Lunch

Blackened Tuna Salad—K-Paul started it all!

2 tablespoons ground black pepper

1 teaspoon garlic powder

⅛ teaspoon dried thyme

¼ teaspoon lemon pepper

¼ teaspoon salt

1 pound fresh tuna steak (about 1-inch-thick),
   cut into 4 equal pieces

3 cups chopped romaine lettuce

¾ cup Balsamic Vinaigrette (page 313)

Mix the black pepper, garlic powder, thyme, lemon pepper, and salt together in a small bowl. Rub the spice mixture all over the tuna to coat. Preheat a medium nonstick skillet over high heat. Add the tuna and sear for about 3 minutes per side. Mound lettuce on 4 salad plates. Top each with seared tuna and drizzle with the vinaigrette.

Serves 4.

Note: New Orleans' own K-Paul started it all, but the blackening craze has now spread nationwide. This is another great dish to make if you have run out of cooking oil—none is needed. Cooking time for the tuna in the recipe yields tuna that is medium-rare, still slightly pink in the center. If you prefer your tuna more well done, cook for an additional 30 seconds per side. You can substitute another meaty fish, such as salmon fillets, or chicken breasts (cook chicken for 4 to 5 minutes a side).

Italian Artichoke Soup—A can't miss recipe.

½ stick butter
¼ cup olive oil
1 medium yellow onion, chopped
5 cloves garlic, peeled and chopped
Three 14-ounce cans artichoke hearts, drained
   and coarsely chopped
5½ cups chicken broth (three 14½-ounce cans)
1 tablespoon chopped fresh parsley
1 teaspoon Italian seasoning
2 tablespoons stone-ground whole-wheat flour
1 cup water
Grated Parmesan cheese, to garnish

Combine the butter and olive oil in a 3-quart saucepan over medium-high heat. When the butter has melted, add the onions and garlic. Sauté until the onions are translucent, about 3 minutes. Add the artichoke hearts, broth, parsley, and Italian seasoning. Bring to a low boil, then reduce the heat to low, cover, and cook for 30 minutes. In a small bowl, dissolve the flour in the water. Stir the mixture into the pot, and raise the heat to medium. Cook, uncovered, for about 15 minutes more, until thickened slightly.

Lunch

Just before serving, sprinkle each bowl of soup with some Parmesan cheese.

Serves 6 to 8.

Note: You can't miss with this garlicky delight, which boasts tasty artichoke hearts floating in a broth seasoned with lots of savory herbs and thickened with a little whole-wheat flour. Canned artichoke hearts work just fine in this recipe, but you could substitute three 10-ounce packages frozen, thawed artichoke hearts if you prefer.

Lunch

No-Cook Chunky Avocado Soup—A California staple.

One 14½-ounce can nonfat chicken broth
2 ripe avocados, peeled
½ cup reduced-fat sour cream, well chilled
½ cup low-fat milk, well chilled
Juice of 1 large lemon
⅛ teaspoon cayenne pepper
1 teaspoon salt
¼ cup chopped white onion
¼ cup finely chopped fresh cilantro

Place the can of broth in the freezer for 10 minutes to chill. Meanwhile, remove the pits from the avocados. Mash 1½ of them, and cut the remaining ½ avocado into cubes. In a medium bowl, mix together the mashed avocado, sour cream, milk, lemon juice, cayenne pepper, and salt. Stir in 1 cup of the chilled broth. Put the avocado and broth mixture into the freezer for a few minutes more, until well chilled, if necessary. Divide among 4 chilled soup bowls and garnish with avocado cubes, chopped onion, and chopped cilantro.

Serves 4.

Note: Avocados, which are high in monounsaturated fat (the good kind of fat), are the primary ingredient of this straight from the freezer to the table soup. Be sure to buy nonfat (defatted) chicken broth, since this soup is not cooked.

Lunch

Quick-Draw Black Bean Soup—"Gunslinger" soup!

4 ounces ham (not sugar-cured), trimmed and
    cut into ¼-inch cubes (optional)
One 15-ounce can black beans, rinsed and
    drained
One 19-ounce can black bean soup
One 14½-ounce can chicken broth
1 tablespoon chili powder
1 medium yellow onion, chopped
2 cloves garlic, crushed
Salt and ground black pepper to taste
Chopped green onion tops or chopped fresh
    cilantro, to garnish

If you wish to add ham to the soup, first brown
it evenly in a 2-quart nonstick saucepan over
medium-high heat, 4 to 5 minutes. Add the
beans, bean soup, broth, chili powder, onion, and
garlic. Bring to a low boil, then reduce the heat
to medium-low, and simmer until the onions
are tender, about 5 minutes. Salt and pepper to
taste. Ladle into soup bowls, and garnish with
green onion tops or cilantro.

Serves 4 to 6.

Note: Canned beans usually have a higher gly-cemic index than home-cooked dried black beans, but we provide this quick-on-the-draw recipe for those occasions when you just don't have time to start from scratch. Take care to rinse and drain the beans well to ensure that no metallic taste from the can lingers. If you do have some cooked black beans on hand and would prefer to use them (see pages 25–27 for di-rections on soaking and cooking dried beans), substitute 2 cups for the canned beans in the recipe.

Lunch

Traditional Black Bean Soup—Solamente Frijoles Negros.

1 pound dried black beans, picked over
⅓ cup olive oil
1 large white onion, chopped, plus additional,
   to garnish
5 cloves garlic, peeled
1 green bell pepper, cored, seeded, and chopped
½ tablespoon dried oregano
8 cups water
2 tablespoons white vinegar
½ tablespoon ground cumin
1 tablespoon plus 1 teaspoon salt
1 teaspoon ground black pepper
2 teaspoons green hot sauce

Put the beans into a large bowl. Add sufficient water to cover by 2 inches and let soak overnight at room temperature. Drain the beans. Heat the oil in a Dutch oven over medium-high heat. Add the onion and sauté until slightly browned, about 5 minutes. Add the garlic and continue to sauté until it gives off an aroma, about 30 seconds. Stir in the bell pepper, beans, oregano, and the 8 cups water. Bring to a boil, then reduce the heat to low, cover, and simmer until the beans are tender, about 1 hour. Stir in the vinegar and cumin and cook for 5 minutes more. Add the salt, black pepper, and hot sauce. Remove about 4 cups of the soup to a food processor or blender, purée, and stir back into the pot. Serve immediately.

Serves 6 to 8.

Note: Beans are a great source of fiber, carbohydrates, and protein—try working them into your diet in place of white rice, white potatoes, and white bread. Preparing dried beans from scratch takes a bit of planning, but not much in the way of hands-on time in the kitchen. Just remember to let them soak overnight and put them up to cook about an hour before starting the recipe in which you will use them. Partially puréeing this soup just before serving lends a smooth, rich texture. If you have a handheld immersible blender, you can do the job right in the pot.

Lunch

Garlic–White Bean Soup—Two winning ingredients.

20 garlic cloves, peeled
1¾ cups chicken broth (one 14½-ounce can)
2 cups cooked navy beans or one 15-ounce can
   navy beans, rinsed and drained
2 tablespoons crumbled goat cheese
3 tablespoons lemon juice
½ teaspoon dry sherry
½ teaspoon dried thyme
Salt and ground black pepper to taste
Chopped fresh cilantro, to garnish

Put the garlic and broth in a 2-cup microwave-safe bowl. Cover and microwave at full power for about 10 minutes, until steamy. Transfer the contents of the bowl to a blender or food processor. Add the beans, goat cheese, lemon juice, sherry, and thyme. Purée and return the purée to the bowl. Microwave at full power until heated through, about 4 minutes. Salt and pepper to taste and garnish with chopped cilantro.

Serves 4.

Note: These two winning ingredients yield such a tasty and healthy soup that you could probably eat it five days a week. (Finding someone to kiss you could be another matter!) Because of the intense garlic flavor, serve this soup in small portions as a first course. You can whip it up in 15 minutes without even turning on the stove. Use home-cooked dried beans (see soaking and cooking directions on pages 25–27), or canned beans in a pinch. You could easily substitute cannellini beans for navy beans.

Chicken Soup with Tomatoes and Green Beans—Everybody's staple.

3⅔ cups chicken broth (two 14½-ounce cans)
One 14½-ounce can diced tomatoes
1 medium yellow onion, chopped
½ stalk celery, chopped
¼ teaspoon dried basil
¼ teaspoon ground white pepper plus
    additional to taste
One 8-ounce package frozen green beans
Salt to taste

Combine the broth, tomatoes, onion, celery, basil, and white pepper in a 3-quart saucepan. Bring to a boil, then add the frozen green beans. Reduce the heat to medium-low, cover, and cook for about 30 minutes, until the vegetables are tender. Add salt and more white pepper to taste.

Serves 6.

Note: Good ol' chicken soup is the staple in just about every kitchen around the world—from homes to VIP gatherings. Here it's served with tomatoes and green beans. If you use frozen beans, don't thaw before adding to the soup—they will be cooked perfectly when the soup is done. To put a little extra flavor in clear broths, add some finely chopped green onions, including the tops, or even small bits of chicken, steak, or other meat.

Lunch

Simple Chicken Soup—Easy but healthy.

5½ cups chicken broth (three 14½-ounce cans)
2 tablespoons reduced-sodium soy sauce
2 medium yellow squash, sliced
1 medium yellow onion, sliced
2 stalks celery, sliced
Salt and ground black pepper to taste

Bring the broth to a boil in a large saucepan. Stir in the soy sauce. Add the squash, onion, and celery. Reduce the heat to low, cover, and cook until the vegetables are tender, about 15 minutes. Add salt and pepper to taste, and serve.

Serves 4.

Note: An easy way to enjoy a light, healthy lunch. Substitute zucchini for the yellow squash, if preferred. If you have any leftover chicken in the fridge, cube it, and add it with the vegetables.

Lunch

French Onion Soup—Bless the French for this one.

1 tablespoon butter
3 large yellow onions, very thinly sliced
1 teaspoon balsamic vinegar
3⅔ cups beef broth (two 14½-ounce cans)
½ cup whole-wheat croutons
¼ cup grated Parmesan cheese

Preheat a nonstick Dutch oven over medium-high heat. Add the butter and onions. When the butter has melted, stir, cover, and cook until the onions are limp and beginning to brown, 4 to 5 minutes. Stir in the vinegar. Add the broth, and bring to a boil. Reduce the heat to low, re-cover, and cook for 20 minutes more. Divide the croutons among 4 warmed soup bowls, ladle the soup on top, and sprinkle 1 tablespoon Parmesan cheese over each.

Serves 4.

Note: Use either homemade beef broth (see page 28) or canned for this soup. Be sure to cook the onions until they are golden brown and slightly caramelized to bring out their natural sweetness; the addition of balsamic vinegar boosts the sweetness even more. If your market doesn't carry whole-wheat croutons, make your own by toasting 2 slices of stone-ground whole-wheat bread, trimming off the crusts, and cutting into the desired size croutons.

Gazpacho Soup—Warm weather fare.

2 large tomatoes, peeled, seeded, and cut into
    chunks
1 medium green bell pepper, seeded and cut
    into chunks
1 medium yellow onion, cut into chunks
½ cucumber, peeled, seeded, and cut into
    chunks
1 clove garlic, peeled
1 tablespoon plus 1 teaspoon red wine vinegar
1 tablespoon olive oil
¼ teaspoon Tabasco or other hot sauce
1 teaspoon salt
½ cup reduced-fat sour cream
1 ripe avocado, peeled, pitted, and cubed

Combine the tomatoes, bell pepper, onion, cucumber, garlic, vinegar, oil, hot sauce, and salt in
a blender or food processor. Purée, pour into a
large bowl, cover, and chill in the freezer for 30
minutes or in the refrigerator for at least 2 hours.
Divide among 4 soup bowls. Float dollops of sour
cream and cubes of avocado in each bowl.

Serves 4.

Note: Primarily a vegetarian dish, it is healthy and not too filling. If you use a hothouse cucumber, you won't have to bother with seeding it. (The seeds in other cucumbers could impart a bitter taste.) Puréeing in a blender will produce a smoother soup than doing so in a food processor.

Green Chili and Jalapeño Soup—
A combination of two tasty peppers.

1 tablespoon olive oil

¼ cup chopped white onion

1 clove garlic, peeled

Two 14½-ounce cans chicken broth

One 10¾-ounce can cream of mushroom soup

One 10¾-ounce can cream of chicken soup

2 cups low-fat milk

Two 4-ounce cans chopped green chilies

2 canned pickled jalapeño peppers, cored,
    seeded, and chopped

½ teaspoon ground cumin

½ pound Velveeta cheese, roughly chopped

1 cup cubed or shredded cooked chicken

1 tablespoon finely chopped fresh cilantro

½ teaspoon salt

⅛ teaspoon ground white pepper

1 lime, cut into 6 wedges

Preheat a Dutch oven over medium heat. Add
the oil and onion and cook, stirring constantly,
until the onion turns translucent, about 5 minutes. Press in the garlic and cook for 30 seconds.
Add the broth, soups, milk, green chilies, jalapeño peppers, and cumin. Cook for 10 minutes,

Lunch

stirring frequently. Add the cheese and cook, still stirring frequently, for about 5 minutes, until melted. Stir in the chicken, cilantro, salt, and white pepper. Cook for about 2 minutes more to warm through. Ladle into 6 bowls and serve each with a lime wedge on the side.

Serves 6 to 8.

Note: Key limes, if you can find them, are the best for flavoring fresh soups. They are the same limes that grow in Mexico and are ever-present on tables in the good, south-of-the-border restaurants.

*Sweet Potato Soup—As nutritious as soup
can get!*

3 large sweet potatoes, scrubbed

4 tablespoons butter

1 large white onion, chopped

1 bunch green onions, trimmed to 2 inches of
   green top and chopped

5½ cups chicken broth (three 14½-ounce cans)

1 teaspoon salt

¾ teaspoon ground black pepper

3 tablespoons stone-ground whole-wheat flour

2½ cups light cream

Poke the sweet potatoes with the tines of a fork.
Microwave at full power until soft, about 8 minutes, turning the potatoes over after 4 minutes.
Let cool enough to handle, peel, and mash in
a medium bowl. Preheat a Dutch oven over
medium heat. Add the butter, onion, and green
onions, and cook, stirring constantly, until the
onions turn translucent, about 3 minutes. Add
the sweet potatoes and cook, stirring, for 1 minute. Stir in the broth and cook for 10 minutes.
Season with salt and pepper. Whisking constantly, slowly add the flour to the soup. Whisk

Lunch

in the cream, cook for 1 minute more to warm through, and serve.

Serves 8.

Note: This is just about as healthy a soup as you can get, since sweet potatoes are one of the most nutritious vegetables in the world. One 4-ounce sweet potato contains 249 percent of the recommended daily allowance of vitamin A (beta-carotene). Since sweet potatoes have a moderate glycemic index, you should not eat them every day if you are trying to lose weight.

Cool Tomato and Cucumber Soup—The hot sauce makes the difference.

2 large cucumbers, peeled, seeded, and chopped
4 cups tomato juice
1 cup plain low-fat or nonfat yogurt
2 teaspoons LOUISIANA Hot Sauce or other
    red hot sauce
1 teaspoon Worcestershire sauce
1 teaspoon salt
¼ teaspoon ground black pepper
1 ripe avocado
1 lemon or lime, cut into 6 wedges

Combine the cucumbers and tomato juice in a food processor or blender and purée. Pour into a large bowl. Stir in the yogurt, hot sauce, Worcestershire sauce, salt, and pepper. Chill in the freezer for 20 minutes. While the soup chills, peel the avocado, remove the pit, and cut into cubes. Divide the soup among 6 chilled bowls, and float a few avocado cubes in each. Serve with a lemon or lime wedge on the side.

Serves 6.

Note: Like many spicy soups, it's best with a squeeze of lemon or lime juice added just prior

to eating, so serve a wedge with each bowl.
Check to make sure that the yogurt you are
buying is one that has had no sugar added. If you
purée the cucumbers and tomato juice in a
large-capacity (8 cups or more) food processor
rather than a smaller blender, you can finish the
soup right in the processor—just add the remaining ingredients, and pulse a few times to
blend.

Tortillaless Soup—The corn is gone!

3⅔ cups chicken broth (two 14½-ounce cans)

One 10-ounce can RO•TEL or diced tomatoes
    and chilies, liquid reserved

1 canned pickled jalapeño pepper, seeded, and
    chopped

1 clove garlic, mashed

½ teaspoon ground cumin

¼ teaspoon ground coriander

Salt to taste

4 Finn Crisps, lightly crushed

¼ cup chopped fresh cilantro

Combine the broth, tomatoes, jalapeño pepper, garlic, cumin, and coriander in a 2-quart sauce-pan. Bring to a low boil over medium-high heat. Reduce the heat to low and taste the soup, adding salt if necessary. Garnish servings with the crushed Finn Crisps and cilantro. Serve immediately.

Serves 4.

Note: All the zip of your favorite tortilla soup— but without the corn tortillas, which have a high-glycemic index. In lieu of the tortillas, crumble Finn Crisps, which are made from rye flour with sesame seeds, or your own favorite whole-grain cracker into the soup. For those who like things a little less spicy, cut down on the amount of pickled jalapeño you use (some brands pack quite a punch), and substitute regular canned tomatoes for the seasoned tomatoes.

VI | Dinner

After a long, busy day a good nutritious dinner that is quick and easy to prepare certainly is appreciated not only by the cook but also by all who eat it. Since dinner is often the largest, most savory meal of the day, this important meal should be well-balanced and include the necessary food groups that you may have missed during a hectic day.

SUGAR BUSTERS! is for every member of your family, especially your children. Today in America almost one half of all children are overweight. Following the SUGAR BUSTERS! lifestyle will improve your entire family's health now and in the future. Proper food in your pantry leads to better choices for overall eating.

Dinner should be a time when all the family comes together. This is a wonderful opportunity to prepare and serve healthy, flavorful meals which instill good nutritional habits. These SUGAR BUSTERS! recipes make dinner a delicious and relaxing experience.

Remember, since most cholesterol is manufactured at night while you are sleeping, keep your insulin levels low by not snacking later in the evening before going to bed.

SUGAR BUSTERS! Guide to Dinner Planning

Good Dinner Ideas	*Dinner Foods to Avoid*
Milk, juices with no sugar added, iced tea with no sugar added, artificially sweetened lemonade, diet colas—all liquids in moderation at mealtime, even water	Sugar-sweetened juices, iced tea, lemonade, and colas
Red wine, preferably, or white wine, in moderation	Cocktails made with mixers that contain sugar; beer

Dinner

Homemade dips and spreads made without sugar, fresh shellfish hors d'oeuvres, fresh vegetable hors d'oeuvres	Commercial dips and spreads made with sugar, breaded seafood hors d'oeuvres, commercially prepared canapés made with white flour
Whole-grain crackers	Regular crackers, rice cakes
Homemade soups and commercial soups with no sugar or white flour added	Corn- and potato-based soups, rice soups, soups with sugar or white flour added
Fresh lettuce, spinach, and vegetable salads with homemade salad dressing made with no sugar or commercial dressings with less than 3 grams of sugar	Prepared deli salads made with sugar; commercial salad dressings with more than 3 grams of sugar
Stone-ground (coarse) semolina pasta dishes	White flour pasta dishes

Brown rice or brown basmati rice, in moderation	White rice
Trimmed lean meats and skinned poultry	Fatty meats and poultry skin, cold cuts with sugar added
All nonbreaded seafood	
Broiled tomatoes, mushrooms, beans and lentils, sweet potatoes, in moderation	French fries, baked and other white and red potatoes, corn
Most fresh, frozen, and canned vegetables	Beets, carrots, parsnips, turnips, and frozen or canned vegetables with sugar added
Whole-grain and stone-ground whole-wheat breads, pumpernickel	White bread, French bread, Italian bread
Stone-ground whole-wheat tortillas	Corn and white flour tortillas

Most fresh fruit (including apricots, grapefruit, cherries, dates, strawberries, blueberries, kiwis, apples, peaches, nectarines, tangerines, oranges, mangoes, and grapes)

Pineapples, raisins, ripe bananas, watermelons

Naturally sweetened frozen or canned fruit with no sugar added

Frozen fruit with sugar added, canned fruit in syrup

Nuts, cheese, sugar-free ice cream

Cookies, cake, regular ice cream

Dinner Recipes

Holiday Birds, page 155

Cabbage Patch Supper, page 157

Cajun Pot Roast, page 159

Chicken and Cheese Enchiladas, page 161

Curried Chicken on Brown Rice, page 163

Orange Ginger Chicken, page 165

Oriental Grilled Chicken, page 166

Quick Chili, page 167

SUGAR BUSTERS! Fajitas, page 168

Quick Skillet-Grilled Fish, page 170

Succulent Baked Fish, page 171

Trout Amandine, page 173

Hamburger Steak, page 175

Horseradish Burger, page 176

Broiled Lamb Chops, page 177

Curried Lamb, page 178

Herb-Crusted Lamb, page 180

Lamb Stew, page 181

Spinach Lasagna, page 183

Mexican Lasagna, page 186

Meatless Chili, page 188

Sautéed Oysters, page 190

Grilled Pork Tender, page 191

Roast Pork with Mustard, page 193

Stuffed Pork Loin, page 194

Grilled Salmon, page 195

Poached Salmon, page 196

Sautéed Shrimp, page 198

Flank Steak, page 199

Ginger Marinated Sirloins, page 201

Smothered Round Steak, page 202

Texas Steak, page 203

Turkey Supreme, page 205

Veal Marsala, page 207

Veal Piccata, page 208

Veal Scaloppine with Tomatoes, page 210

Veal Chops, page 212

Dinner

Holiday Birds—This recipe is great any time of the year.

1 dozen quail (or dove)
2 tablespoons canola or olive oil
Salt to taste
1 cup stone-ground whole-wheat flour
¼ cup bacon drippings
½ cup chopped yellow onion
1 cup sliced white button mushrooms
1 cup dry white wine
½ cup heavy cream
Chopped fresh parsley, to garnish

Rub the birds all over with oil and salt. Place them in a bag, and shake to coat with flour. Brown the birds in the bacon drippings, in batches if necessary, in a large, heavy (preferably cast-iron) skillet over medium-high heat, about 5 minutes, turning as needed for even browning. Remove the birds to a platter and stir the onions and mushrooms into the pan drippings. Stirring constantly, cook for 1 minute. Return the birds to the skillet. Add the wine. Cover, reduce the heat to low, and cook until the juices run clear when the birds are pricked with a fork, about 20 minutes, adding more wine if necessary.

Dinner

(Another method is to bake the birds in a heavy skillet with an ovenproof handle and covered in a 350-degree oven for almost 20 minutes.) Stir in the cream, and cook on the stove top until slightly thickened, about 2 minutes, turning the birds to coat evenly. Garnish with parsley.

Serves 4 to 6.

Note: Lament the fact you didn't get more birds. This recipe can easily be adapted to other game birds, such as pheasant or Cornish hen.

Dinner

Cabbage Patch Supper—100 percent of your RDA of vitamin C.

1 pound round steak trimmed and cut into
  ½-inch cubes
1 medium yellow onion, chopped
1 medium green bell pepper, cored, seeded, and
  chopped
1 teaspoon canola or olive oil
2 chicken bouillon cubes dissolved in 1 cup
  boiling water
½ teaspoon salt
¼ teaspoon ground black pepper
4 cups coarsely shredded green cabbage

Combine the steak, onion, bell pepper, and oil in a large nonstick skillet. Brown over medium heat, about 5 minutes. Add the liquid bouillon, salt, and black pepper. Reduce the heat to medium-low and cook, stirring frequently, for 5 minutes. Add the cabbage and cook for about 15 minutes more, still stirring frequently, until the cabbage is tender and the liquid has been absorbed.

Serves 4.

Note: You'll get 100 percent of your United States recommended daily allowance (U.S.RDA) for vitamin C with this meal—a cup of cooked cabbage provides 60 percent of the daily allowance, while ¼ cup green bell pepper supplies another 37 percent. Since the onion will supply the rest, why spend your money on a vitamin C capsule? This is a lot more satisfying.

Cajun Pot Roast—This is an extremely versatile and delicious recipe.

For beef, pork, lamb, venison, duck, dove, quail, or, yes, even a mixture of the above!

4 pound beef rump roast
2¼ cups Wish-Bone or other Italian salad dressing
2 tablespoons olive oil
1 teaspoon Season•All or other seasoned salt
1 teaspoon ground black pepper
¼ cup water

Combine the roast and 2 cups of the salad dressing in a large plastic storage bag. Squeeze out excess air, seal tightly, and massage to coat the meat all over. Marinate in the refrigerator for at least 2 hours and up to overnight, turning the roast over at least once. Preheat a heavy (preferably cast-iron) Dutch oven over high heat. Add the oil. Remove the roast from the marinade, and add it to the pan. Brown on all sides, 4 to 5 minutes. Sprinkle the meat with the seasoned salt and pepper. Add the water and the remaining ¼ cup salad dressing. Cover, reduce the heat to low, and cook until very tender, about

3 hours, checking occasionally to see if additional water is needed.

Serves 12 (3 per pound of roast).

Note: Using a tried and true method of flavoring and tenderizing meat—marinating it in Italian salad dressing—this recipe is as versatile as it is simple. We encourage experimentation—try substituting pork, lamb, venison, duck, game birds, or a combination of your favorite meats for the beef. Cook smaller roasts or poultry for only 2 to 2½ hours; game birds may need to cook for only about 2 hours, until the meat begins to fall off the bone. Take care not to let all the liquid in the Dutch oven evaporate or the meat will toughen. If you add more water as the roast cooks, you may want to add a little more seasoning as well.

Chicken and Cheese Enchiladas—Always a great Mexican dish.

1 medium yellow onion, minced
1 clove garlic, minced
¼ cup canola oil
1½ cups tomato sauce
1 teaspoon dried oregano
1 teaspoon salt
1½ cups shredded cooked chicken
½ teaspoon garlic salt
½ teaspoon ground black pepper
Eight 6-inch whole-wheat tortillas
One 4-ounce can whole green chilies, drained
  and cut into ¼-inch strips
2 cups grated cheddar cheese
1 cup reduced-fat sour cream (optional)

Preheat the oven to 350 degrees. Combine the onion, garlic, and 2 tablespoons of the oil in a 1-quart saucepan. Stirring occasionally, cook over medium heat until the onion turns translucent, about 3 minutes. Add the tomato sauce, oregano, and salt. Reduce the heat to low and cook, un-covered, for 15 minutes. Meanwhile, season the chicken with the garlic salt and pepper and put it in a medium nonstick skillet, along with the remaining 2 tablespoons oil. Heat for about 10 minutes over medium-low heat. Remove the meat to a bowl, and warm the tortillas in the same pan for about 15 seconds a side. Divide the chicken and the chilies among the tortillas. Roll the tortillas up and place them in a 9-by-13-inch baking dish that has been coated with cooking spray. Cover with the tomato sauce, and sprinkle with the grated cheese. Cover and bake for about 15 minutes, until the cheese is melted and bubbly. Top with sour cream, if desired.

Serves 4.

Note: The enchiladas can be made with about ½ pound prebrowned ground beef in place of the chicken for variety. Or you can skip the meat and simply double the amount of cheese.

Curried Chicken on Brown Rice—East Indians like a chicken curry for good reason.

½ cup chopped yellow onion
½ cup chopped celery
2 tablespoons canola oil
¼ cup stone-ground whole-wheat flour
1¾ cups chicken broth (one 14½-ounce can)
2 cups cubed cooked chicken
¼ cup tomato juice
1 teaspoon Worcestershire sauce
1 to 2 teaspoons curry powder (to taste)
Salt to taste
2 cups cooked brown rice

Combine the onion, celery, and oil in a medium nonstick skillet. Stirring constantly, cook over medium heat until softened, about 3 minutes. Add the flour and stir for 1 minute. Add the broth and continue to cook and stir until the mixture bubbles and is somewhat thickened, about 2 minutes. Add the chicken, tomato juice, Worcestershire sauce, curry powder, and salt. Still stirring constantly, cook for 3 minutes more to allow the flavors to blend. Serve over the brown rice.

Serves 4 to 6.

Note: Actually a blend of several spices, including turmeric, which lends the familiar yellow
hue, curry powder is the main component of a
range of spicy and savory Indian dishes. For a
hotter, more typically East Indian curry, increase the amount of curry powder a bit and add
a teaspoon of cayenne pepper, or choose a
more potent Madras curry instead of a milder
variety. Use leftover chicken or one of the
handy precooked varieties now found in most
supermarkets.

Dinner

Orange Ginger Chicken—A flavorful chicken dish.

½ cup orange juice
½ cup soy sauce
1 teaspoon grated orange zest (peel)
1 teaspoon ground ginger
½ teaspoon onion powder
One 3½ pound frying chicken, quartered

Combine the orange juice, soy sauce, orange zest, ginger, and onion powder in a large plastic storage bag. Add the chicken, squeeze out excess air, seal tightly, and massage to coat the chicken all over. Marinate in the refrigerator for at least 2 hours and up to overnight. Preheat a broiler or set up a grill. Remove the chicken from the marinade and broil or grill for about 15 minutes a side, until the chicken reaches an internal temperature of 170 degrees and the juices run clear when pricked with a fork.

Serves 4.

Note: This flavorful dish pairs well with stir-fried or sautéed vegetables. For maximum flavor—and convenience—make the marinade a day ahead and let the chicken marinate overnight in the refrigerator.

Oriental Grilled Chicken—A Far East offering.

½ teaspoon onion powder
½ teaspoon garlic salt
2 tablespoons finely chopped flat-leaf parsley
4 large skinless chicken breasts
1 cup soy sauce
Juice of 1 lemon

Sprinkle the onion powder, garlic salt, and parsley on the chicken breasts and put them into a plastic storage bag. Add the soy sauce and lemon juice. Squeeze out excess air, seal tightly, and massage to work the marinade into the chicken. Place in the refrigerator and marinate for 4 to 6 hours. Set up a grill or preheat a broiler. Remove the chicken from the marinade and grill or broil for at least 6 minutes a side until the breasts are cooked through.

Serves 4.

Note: A seasoned soy sauce mixture gives this simple dish a teriyaki-like taste. We like the added flavor lent by outdoor grilling, but broiling will allow you to enjoy the chicken in more inclement weather.

Quick Chili—A great winter dish.

1 pound lean ground beef chuck
1 medium yellow onion, chopped
½ cup chopped green bell pepper
1½ cups cooked pinto beans (one 15-ounce can,
    rinsed and drained)
Two 10-ounce cans RO•TEL diced tomatoes
    and chilies, drained
2 tablespoons chili powder
1 tablespoon ground cumin
1 teaspoon salt

Combine the ground meat, onion, and bell pepper in a medium saucepan. Stirring constantly, cook over medium-high heat until the meat is crumbly and the onion translucent, about 5 minutes. Add the beans, tomatoes, chili powder, cumin, and salt. Continue to cook and stir until the chili is bubbly, about 4 minutes.

Serves 4.

Note: There are an infinite number of ways to make chili. You can make it with or without beans, with a lot or a little chili powder, and with or without cayenne or other hot peppers. Cook it to suit your taste. At any rate, chili makes for a very savory meal.

Dinner

Dinner

SUGAR BUSTERS! Fajitas—A Tex-Mex mainstay.

1½ pounds beef skirt or flank steak, trimmed
    and cut into ½-inch strips

Fajitas Marinade:

½ cup soy sauce
½ cup canola oil
¼ cup red wine vinegar
6 cloves garlic, minced
1 green onion, minced
1 teaspoon ground black pepper
½ teaspoon salt
One medium yellow onion, sliced into thin
    wedges
One green bell pepper, cored, seeded, and cut
    into strips

Put the steak into a large plastic storage bag.
Add the soy sauce, oil, vinegar, garlic, green
onion, black pepper, and salt. Squeeze out excess air, seal tightly, and massage to work the
marinade into the beef. Marinate for 1½ hours
at room temperature or in the refrigerator
overnight. Preheat a large nonstick skillet over
high heat on the stove top or over a grill. Re-

move the meat from the marinade, and add it to the pan, along with the yellow onion and bell pepper. Cook until the meat is cooked through and browned, 4 to 5 minutes.

Serves 4.

Note: You can easily substitute 1½ pounds skinless, boneless chicken breasts or peeled and deveined shrimp (cook the shrimp just until they turn pink) for the beef in this low-glycemic Tex-Mex mainstay. It's great with guacamole salad (see page 106), pinto beans (see page 240), and salsa—either homemade (see page 324) or your favorite prepared variety. If you must, serve with 2 whole-wheat tortillas per serving.

Quick Skillet-Grilled Fish—If consumed immediately, this is the best of the best.

Four 6-ounce fresh nonoily white fish fillets
½ teaspoon garlic salt
1 large lemon, halved
2 tablespoons olive oil
2 tablespoons chopped fresh flat-leaf parsley

Sprinkle the fillets with garlic salt. Squeeze lemon juice generously over the fish. Pour the oil into the bottom of a large skillet and preheat over high heat. Add the fillets, and sprinkle with half of the parsley. Cook until the fish is browned on the bottom, about 2 minutes. Turn, sprinkle with the rest of the parsley, and cook for about 2 minutes more, until browned on the second side. Serve immediately.

Serves 4.

Note: Use any nonoily white fish, such as redfish, speckled trout, red snapper, rockfish, or perch. After washing the fish, be sure to dry the fillets thoroughly to prevent spatter when they are put into the hot oil.

Succulent Baked Fish—A delicate fish with a savory flavor.

Salt to taste
Eight 4-ounce fresh nonoily white fish fillets
1 large lemon, cut into 8 wedges
1 large yellow onion, minced
1 large clove garlic, minced
½ cup chopped green bell pepper
2 medium tomatoes, each cut into 8 wedges
¼ cup dry white wine
¼ cup olive oil
Salt to taste
Ground black pepper to taste
½ teaspoon dried oregano

Preheat the oven to 400 degrees. Lightly salt each fish fillet and roll it up around a lemon wedge, using toothpicks to secure in place. Scatter the onion, garlic, and bell pepper over the bottom of a 2-quart glass baking dish. Arrange the fish rolls and the tomato wedges on top. Drizzle the wine and oil over the contents of the dish. Sprinkle with salt, pepper, and oregano. Bake for about 20 minutes, until tender, basting at least once with pan juices. Serve 2 fish rolls per person with vegetables scattered on top.

Serves 4.

Note: Use any nonoily white fish, such as redfish, speckled trout, red snapper, rockfish, or perch. For lemon wedges just the right size to roll the fish fillets up around, quarter the lemon the long way and then cut each quarter in half crosswise.

Dinner

Trout Amandine—Another all time New Orleans favorite.

¼ cup stone-ground whole-wheat flour
1 teaspoon salt
1 teaspoon paprika
Six 5- to 6-ounce speckled or rainbow trout
   fillets
1 teaspoon olive oil
3 tablespoons butter, melted
½ cup sliced almonds
Juice of ½ lemon
6 drops LOUISIANA or other hot sauce
1 tablespoon chopped fresh parsley

Mix together the flour, salt, and paprika and coat the fillets on both sides with the mixture. Spread the olive oil over the bottom of a 17-by-11-inch baking pan and lay the fillets in it skin-side down. Pour 2 tablespoons of the butter over the fish. Position the dish about 4 inches from the heat source and broil until browned on the outside and opaque at the center, 4 to 5 minutes. Meanwhile, combine the almonds and the remaining 1 tablespoon butter in a medium nonstick skillet. Stirring constantly, cook over medium heat until browned, about 3 minutes. Remove the pan from the heat, and stir in the lemon juice, hot sauce, and parsley. Plate the fillets, and spoon some of the almond mixture over each.

Serves 6.

Note: The secret to gourmet-tasting fish is to serve it fresh and hot, not kept warm in an oven or under a heat lamp. Short of catching the fish yourself, for the freshest fillets possible buy a whole fish, and have your fish merchant clean and fillet it for you.

*Hamburger Steak—Serve as a meat dish and
not on a bun.*

2 pounds lean ground beef chuck
1 small yellow onion, chopped
¼ cup chopped fresh parsley
½ teaspoon black pepper
1 teaspoon salt

Put the ground beef into a large bowl and mix
in the onion, parsley, and pepper. Form 6 thick
patties from the mixture. In batches, put the
patties into a large nonstick skillet, sprinkle
with salt, and cook over medium heat 5 minutes a side for medium or 7 minutes a side for
well-done (but dry!).

Serves 6.

Note: Serve the hamburger steak with your favorite steak sauce on the side or topped with
Béarnaise Sauce (see page 315 for homemade).
It's great with Sautéed Mushrooms (page 258)
and with a Caesar salad (use the dressing on
page 307).

Horseradish Burger—A burger with a kick.

1 pound lean ground beef chuck
½ cup chopped yellow onion
1 tablespoon prepared horseradish
1 tablespoon prepared yellow mustard
1 tablespoon tomato sauce
½ teaspoon salt (or more to taste)

In a medium bowl, combine the ground meat, onion, horseradish, mustard, tomato sauce, and salt. Mix well and form into 4 patties. Place in a large nonstick skillet and cook over medium heat to desired doneness, 3 to 4 minutes a side for medium-rare, 6 minutes if you prefer your burgers well-done (but dry!).

Serves 4.

Note: You can add a tremendous variety of spices to the raw ground beef and have the result come out very well. For "onion and tomato buns," an alternative to high-glycemic hamburger buns, dip onion and tomato slices in egg white and coat with grated Parmesan cheese. Brown in oil over high heat until crisped and lightly browned, about 1 minute a side. Sprinkle with pepper and seasoned salt. Serve each burger between an onion slice and a tomato slice.

Dinner

*Broiled Lamb Chops—Our ancestors ate a lot
of lamb! This is a quick but tasty entrée.*

Four 5-ounce loin lamb chops
1 tablespoon lemon juice
2 teaspoons apple cider vinegar
½ teaspoon Italian seasoning
¼ teaspoon garlic salt
¼ teaspoon ground black pepper

Preheat the broiler. Drizzle the chops on both
sides with lemon juice and vinegar. In a small
bowl, mix together the Italian seasoning, garlic
salt, and pepper. Sprinkle the mixture onto both
sides of each chop to coat. Place the chops in a
broiler pan and broil for about 4 minutes a side
for medium doneness.

Serves 2.

Note: This recipe tastes great cooked over your
outdoor grill. Cooking times vary by altitude.
The higher the altitude, the longer it takes to
even boil water. So, if you live in the high
mountains and you are cooking over a wood or
charcoal fire, you need to add a couple of minutes to the cooking time to get your meats to
the doneness you desire. In addition to broiling
or grilling, you could also cook the chops on the
stove top, in a large nonstick skillet for about
5 minutes a side over medium heat.

Dinner

Curried Lamb—Lamb and curry were meant for each other.

1 pound lean lamb leg meat, trimmed and cut into ¼-inch cubes
2 teaspoons curry powder
½ teaspoon salt
½ teaspoon ground black pepper
1 tablespoon canola oil
1 medium yellow onion, chopped
1 tablespoon chopped fresh flat-leaf parsley
½ cup water
3 cups cooked brown rice

Combine the lamb, curry powder, salt, and pepper in a bowl, and toss to coat the meat. Transfer to a large nonstick skillet along with the oil and onion. Stirring constantly, cook over high heat until the meat is lightly browned, 4 to 5 minutes. Add the parsley and water and stir well. Cover, reduce the heat to medium-low, and cook for about 10 minutes, until the meat is cooked through and a thick sauce has formed. Serve over warm brown rice.

Serves 4.

Note: This is a nice mellow meat curry, much like they make it in the Caribbean. If you have a taste for something a bit hotter and spicier, try boosting the amount of curry powder gradually and adding some cayenne pepper in ½ teaspoon increments. For 3 cups of cooked brown rice, start with 1 cup dry rice and cook according to package directions.

Herb-Crusted Lamb—A simple, yet rewarding way to eat lamb.

3 tablespoons chopped fresh parsley
1 tablespoon finely chopped green onion
2 teaspoons finely chopped garlic
2 tablespoons olive oil
⅓ cup whole-wheat bread crumbs
½ teaspoon ground cumin
½ teaspoon ground turmeric
½ teaspoon dried thyme
Salt and ground black pepper to taste
Four 6-ounce pieces loin of lamb

Preheat the oven to 425 degrees. Combine the parsley, green onion, garlic, oil, bread crumbs, cumin, turmeric, thyme, salt, and pepper on a plate. Stir to mix. Press the seasoning mixture onto both sides of each piece of lamb and place in an 8-inch square glass baking dish. Bake, turning the pieces of lamb once, for a total of 15 minutes for medium-rare doneness or 20 minutes for medium doneness.

Serves 4.

Note: This is the most tender cut of lamb. Buy 4 loin lamb chops and remove the bones. Cut off the outer layer of fat before cooking.

Lamb Stew—Let your stove top do the work!

2 tablespoons butter
1 large white onion, chopped
1½ pounds lamb stew meat
½ teaspoon dried thyme
½ teaspoon dried rosemary
½ teaspoon salt
⅛ teaspoon ground black pepper
1 cup chicken broth
One 9-ounce package frozen cut green beans,
    thawed
One 9-ounce package frozen baby peas, thawed

Melt the butter in a large nonstick saucepan over medium heat. Add the onion and sauté just until softened, about 2 minutes. Stir in the lamb, thyme, rosemary, salt, and pepper. Pour in the broth and bring to a boil. Cover, reduce the heat to low, and simmer until the meat is tender, about 1½ hours. Stir in the beans and peas and cook for 10 minutes more.

Serves 4 to 6.

Note: While you can't cook this meal in half an hour, there's little prepping involved in the hearty stew if you use precut lamb stew meat and frozen green beans and peas. Just chop an onion, and let your stove top do the work while you take care of other interests. If you prefer slightly leaner lamb leg meat, cut into 1½-inch cubes, and cook for about 30 minutes longer.

Dinner

Spinach Lasagna

1 package Owens Farm or other sausage
Two 10-ounce packages frozen cut spinach
Two 26-ounce jars no-sugar-added tomato
  sauce
One 15-ounce part skim Ricotta cheese
2 large eggs
1 box whole-wheat lasagna noodles
1 small box of fresh sliced mushrooms
2 cups shredded mozzarella cheese
Grated Parmesan cheese to taste

Preheat oven to 350 degrees. Brown sausage in a medium nonstick skillet over medium-high heat, 5 to 7 minutes, stirring to break up. Meanwhile, place the packages of spinach into a microwave oven and microwave at full power for 7 minutes. Remove to a colander and drain. Mix together the tomato sauce, ricotta cheese, and eggs. Spread a thin layer of the sauce mixture over the bottom of a 9-by-13-inch lasagna pan. Top with a layer of uncooked lasagna noodles, another layer of sauce, a layer of spinach, a layer of sausage, a layer of mushrooms, a layer of mozzarella cheese, and a layer of lightly sprinkled Parmesan cheese. Repeat all 8 layers. Cover with foil and bake for about 1 hour, until bubbly. Remove from oven and let stand for 15 minutes before slicing. Enjoy!

Serves 6.

Note: This is the favorite recipe of Pam Hoffman of New Orleans. While it takes a little longer to cook, Pam says it is extremely easy for a dish that provides such good results—both in taste and in providing success on the SUGAR BUSTERS! lifestyle. Pam has lost over 110 pounds! See her before and after pictures on the next page.

Dinner

Pam Hoffman, before
SUGAR BUSTERS!

Pam Hoffman, after.

Mexican Lasagna—A south-of-the-border treat.

1 pound ground pork
1 small yellow onion, chopped
1 large garlic clove, chopped
One 10-ounce can RO•TEL diced tomatoes
   with chilies, drained
½ tablespoon chili powder
1 cup part-skim milk ricotta cheese
1 large egg, beaten
2 tablespoons chopped fresh cilantro
Three 9-inch whole-wheat tortillas
¾ cup shredded mozzarella cheese

Preheat the oven to 400 degrees. Preheat a large nonstick skillet over high heat. Add the pork, onion, and garlic. Stirring and breaking up the meat with a fork, cook until the pork is crumbly and no longer pink, 2 to 3 minutes. Reduce the heat to medium. Add the tomatoes and chili powder and cook until thickened, about 2 minutes. Meanwhile, mix together the ricotta cheese, egg, and cilantro in a bowl. Place a tortilla in the bottom of a 9-inch round cake pan. Spread the meat mixture over the tortilla. Add a second tortilla and spread the ricotta mixture on top. Add the third tortilla, cover with aluminum foil, and bake for 15 minutes. Remove the foil, scatter with the mozzarella cheese, and bake until the cheese has melted and the tortilla is lightly browned, about 5 minutes.

Serves 4.

Note: There's no need to bother with cooking lasagna noodles when you make this fast but filling version. Substitute ground beef or a pork and beef mixture for the pork if you like, but make sure to use whole-wheat tortillas rather than high-glycemic corn or flour tortillas.

Meatless Chili—A chili to satisfy most vegetarians.

3 medium yellow onions, chopped
2 cloves garlic, minced
1 tablespoon olive oil
3 large tomatoes, seeded and chopped
One 8-ounce can tomato sauce
One 15½-ounce can pinto or kidney beans,
     rinsed and drained
1 cup water
Juice of ½ lemon
1 tablespoon plus 1 teaspoon dried oregano
2 teaspoons chili powder
¼ teaspoon cayenne pepper
Salt to taste

Combine the onions, garlic, and oil in a 2-quart saucepan over medium heat. Stirring constantly, cook until the onion turns translucent, about 5 minutes. Stir in the tomatoes, tomato sauce, beans, water, lemon juice, oregano, chili powder, and cayenne pepper. Stirring occasionally, cook for 20 minutes; add salt to taste before serving.

Serves 4 to 6.

Note: This chili is high in fiber and low in fat. Fans of hot and spicy foods will love the chili served with cream cheese–stuffed jalapeño peppers on the side. Halve, core, and seed 6 whole canned jalapeño peppers, and fill each with about ½ tablespoon cream cheese.

Sautéed Oysters—For those who don't like oysters raw.

2 tablespoons chopped shallot
2 tablespoons butter
1 pint shucked oysters, drained
1 teaspoon Worcestershire sauce
Salt to taste
Juice of ½ lemon

Combine the shallots and butter in a medium skillet, and cook over medium-low heat for about 5 minutes, until translucent. Add the oysters, Worcestershire sauce, and salt. Cook for 6 to 8 minutes, until the edges curl and the oysters are firm to the touch, turning them over once. Squeeze the lemon over the oysters during the last minute of cooking. Serve in shallow bowls.

Serves 2.

Note: If you use smaller, Gulf of Mexico oysters, you can serve them in a chafing dish as an hors d'oeuvre. As an entrée, the oysters are particularly good with a green salad or vegetable, such as green beans, peas, or asparagus.

Dinner

Grilled Pork Tender—The prime cut of pork.

4 strips bacon

2-pound pork tenderloin

½ cup soy sauce

1 tablespoon grated yellow onion

1 clove garlic, chopped

Wrap the bacon strips around the tenderloin and secure with toothpicks. Place in a plastic storage bag. In a small bowl, mix together the soy sauce, onion, and garlic. Pour over the pork, squeeze excess air from the bag, and seal tightly. Marinate overnight in the refrigerator. Preheat a broiler or set up a grill. Remove the meat from the marinade. Position about 4 inches from the heat source and broil or grill for 7 minutes. Turn the tenderloin and cook for 7 minutes more. Turn a final time and cook for about 4 minutes, until the meat has reached an internal temperature of 150 degrees. Remove to a cutting board and let sit for about 5 minutes before slicing. Pour natural juices, if any, over the sliced tenderloin and serve.

Serves 6 to 8.

Note: Pork tenders are versatile and virtually foolproof. They're lean, trimmed, and quick-cooking. No matter how you decide to prepare them, just about the only way to goof up is to overcook the tenders and dry them out.

Dinner

Roast Pork with Mustard—As easy as 1, 2, 3.

¼ cup teriyaki sauce
1 tablespoon plus 1 teaspoon dry white wine
1 tablespoon Dijon mustard
Two ¾-pound pork tenderloins

Preheat the oven to 400 degrees. In a small bowl, mix together the teriyaki sauce, wine, and mustard. Put the tenderloins in a shallow roasting pan and pour the mixture over them. Roast for about 30 minutes, turning midway through, until the tenderloins are well browned and have reached an internal temperature of 150 degrees. Remove to a cutting board and let sit for 3 to 5 minutes before slicing. Drizzle the meat with pan juices and serve.

Serves 4.

Note: This recipe really is as easy as one, two three—sauce, bake, and slice. Small pork tenderloins, vacuum-packed two to a pack, are available in many supermarkets. For variety, try one of the new flavored teriyaki sauces, such as roasted garlic teriyaki, but be sure to choose a brand without a lot of added sugar.

Stuffed Pork Loin—Fresh apricots do the trick here.

One 1-pound boneless pork loin roast, trimmed
¾ to 1 cup chopped fresh apricots
Salt and ground black pepper to taste

Preheat the oven to 450 degrees. Stand the roast upright, and pierce down through the center with a knife. Make a second cut to form an X, then create a cavity in which the apricots can be stuffed by inserting and rotating the handle of a wooden spoon. Stuff with the apricots, and salt and pepper to taste. Roast the pork for 15 minutes. Reduce the oven temperature to 300 degrees, and roast for 15 to 20 minutes more or until the meat has reached an internal temperature of 150 degrees. Remove to a cutting board, and let sit for 3 to 5 minutes before slicing. Cut in ½-inch or 1-inch slices, as desired.

Serves 4.

Note: Another way to prepare the roast is to cut it lengthwise to form a pocket, without cutting the meat completely in half; stuff and then tie with a string to hold the stuffing in place. You could use a similar quantity of chopped fresh peaches or orange segments if you prefer their flavor to that of apricots.

Dinner

Grilled Salmon—A heart-healthy entrée.

3 tablespoons olive oil
1 teaspoon fresh lime juice
1 tablespoon dried marjoram
⅛ teaspoon salt
⅛ teaspoon ground black pepper
Four 6-ounce salmon steaks
1 lime, cut into wedges

Mix together the oil, lime juice, marjoram, salt, and pepper in a small bowl. Brush the salmon steaks all over with the mixture. Set up a grill or preheat a broiler. Position the fish about 4 inches from the heat source and grill or broil the steaks for about 3 minutes per side, until the fish flakes easily, brushing with more lime oil after turning the fish. Decorate each serving with lime wedges.

Serves 4.

Note: Salmon is a very good and natural source of omega-3 fatty acid. It's also rich in calcium, niacin, and potassium.

Poached Salmon—For those who like poached salmon with some added flavor.

2 cups water
1 cup dry white wine
3 sprigs parsley
1 stalk celery, chopped
½-inch strip peeled fresh ginger
1 bay leaf
2 whole black peppercorns
Two 8-ounce salmon steaks
¼ lemon
Salt and ground black pepper to taste

Combine the water, wine, parsley, celery, ginger, bay leaf, and peppercorns in a small, straight-sided skillet. Bring to a boil over medium heat. Cover, reduce the heat to low, and simmer for 5 minutes. Remove and discard the parsley, celery, ginger, and bay leaf. Add the salmon to the pan, re-cover, and simmer for 8 to 10 minutes, until the fish flakes easily. Squeeze lemon over the steaks and season with salt and pepper before serving.

Serves 2.

Note: Use either chinook salmon from the Pacific, coho, or farm-raised Atlantic salmon in this recipe. Increase the amount of fresh ginger (don't substitute ground ginger) and peppercorns to taste. Top with hollandaise sauce (see pages 317 and 318 for homemade) if you like.

Sautéed Shrimp—A "can't miss" treat!

¼ cup olive oil or butter
2 pounds medium shrimp, peeled and deveined
½ cup chopped fresh flat-leaf parsley
1 teaspoon garlic salt
1 lemon

Preheat the oil or melt the butter in a large non-stick skillet over medium heat. Add the shrimp, parsley, and garlic salt. Sauté until the shrimp are opaque, about 2–2½ minutes. Squeeze the lemon over the shrimp and cook for 1 minute more. Plate the shrimp and drizzle with pan juices.

Serves 4.

Note: Shrimp are low in fat and calories, but high in iron and potassium. For a more filling dish, serve over brown rice.

Flank Steak—Makes a very tasty burger.

One 1-pound flank steak
1 teaspoon garlic powder (or to taste)
½ teaspoon salt (or to taste)
1 cup olive oil plus additional for brushing
  buns
6 whole-wheat hamburger buns

Put the steak into a 9-by-13-inch glass baking dish and sprinkle with garlic powder and salt on both sides. Add the oil, cover, and marinate at room temperature for up to 2 hours or in the refrigerator overnight, turning the steak at least once. Preheat a broiler or set up a grill. Remove the steak from the marinade and broil or grill for 4 minutes a side for medium doneness. Brush the inside of the buns lightly with oil, place brushed-side facing the heat source, and toast in the broiler or on the grill. Remove the steak to a cutting board, and thinly slice on the diagonal. Pile several thin slices on each bun. Cut the sandwiches in half, and serve three halves per person.

Serves 4 (1½ sandwiches each).

Note: Flank steak is very lean, but benefits from marinating since it is somewhat fibrous. It is best cooked to no more than a medium doneness and sliced across the grain in thin diagonal slices. Serve with pinto or black beans (see pages 240 and 221) and a green salad.

Dinner

Ginger Marinated Sirloins—Ginger is an often overlooked spice.

2 cups Burgundy or other dry red wine
One 10-ounce bottle soy sauce
2 tablespoons ground ginger
4 garlic cloves, peeled
Four ¾-pound loin strip steaks

Combine the wine, soy sauce, and ginger in a large plastic storage bag. Press in the garlic. Add the steaks, squeeze out excess air, and seal. Marinate for 4 to 6 hours in the refrigerator, turning the steaks at least once. Set up a grill or preheat a broiler. Remove the steaks from the marinade and grill or broil for about 5 minutes a side for medium doneness.

Serves 4.

Note: Serve with beans, asparagus, and a green salad. If you prefer to use fresh ginger, use about 2 tablespoons grated ginger.

Smothered Round Steak (or Venison)—An old and reliable recipe.

One 2-pound round steak or venison backstrap
    (about ¼-inch-thick)
Ground white pepper to taste
2 teaspoons olive oil
2 medium white onions, sliced
1 to 1½ cups water
1 beef bouillon cube

Trim the meat and cut it into 1-by-3-inch slices. Sprinkle with white pepper. Preheat a large non-stick skillet over high heat. Add the oil. In batches if necessary, brown the meat on all sides, about 3 minutes. Add the onions, enough of the water to cover the bottom of the pan by ¼ inch, and the bouillon cube. Cover, reduce the heat to medium-low, and simmer until tender, 20 to 40 minutes, depending upon the cut of meat.

Serves 6 to 8.

Note: By all means use venison in place of beef if you are lucky enough to have some. The pan juices from the dish are very tasty; try serving the meat over cooked whole-wheat noodles and spooning some juices on top.

Texas Steak (sirloin, strip, or filet)
—A twice a year cookout delight.

¾ teaspoon garlic powder

½ teaspoon plus ⅛ teaspoon Lawry's or other
  seasoned salt

½ teaspoon onion salt

¾ teaspoon ground black pepper

One 5-pound sirloin steak (approximately
  3½ inches thick)

1 tablespoon lemon juice

1 teaspoon apple cider vinegar

1 stick butter

Mix together the garlic powder, seasoned salt,
onion salt, and pepper in a small bowl. Drizzle
the steak with the lemon juice and vinegar. Put
the steak on a plate and rub 1¾ teaspoons of the
seasoning mixture into the meat. Cover and
marinate for 2 hours at room temperature or
overnight in the refrigerator. Light up a grill, using mesquite or hickory wood or chips. Remove
the steak from the marinade and position 3 to
3½ inches from the heat source. Grill or broil
with cover closed for 30 to 60 minutes to desired doneness. Time will vary according to the
thickness of the steak and the heat of the fire;

check periodically for desired doneness. It can take longer to cook a steak of this size on an uncovered outdoor grill. Meanwhile, melt the butter in a small saucepan over medium heat, adding the remaining ¾ teaspoon of the seasoning mixture. Slice the steak into ¼-inch-thick strips, drizzle with seasoned butter, and serve immediately. Watch out, Ruth!

Serves 6 to 8.

Note: This dish is designed for the grill and tastes best cooked over a mesquite fire. But if you're rained out and have to broil indoors, this steak will still taste good.

Dinner

Turkey Supreme—The big bird makes a hit.

¼ cup butter

3 tablespoons whole-wheat flour

2 teaspoons salt

½ teaspoon paprika

¼ teaspoon curry powder

¼ teaspoon ground black pepper

2 cups low-fat milk

3 cups diced cooked turkey breast

1 cup sliced or chopped almonds

One 9-ounce package frozen baby peas, thawed, or one 15-ounce can baby peas, rinsed and drained

½ cup half-and-half

8 slices stone-ground whole-wheat bread

Melt the butter in a 3-quart nonstick saucepan over medium heat. Blend in the flour, salt, paprika, curry powder, and pepper. Stir in the milk. Stirring constantly, cook until slightly thickened, about 5 minutes. Add the turkey, almonds, and peas. Reduce the heat to medium-low and cook, uncovered, for 10 minutes. Stir in the half-and-half and cook to heat through, 1 to 2 minutes more. Serve over the toast slices.

Serves 8.

Note: Although low in fat, calories, and cholesterol, turkey is high in protein, phosphorus, and niacin. Make sure to use the tiny sweet variety of peas; there is no need to precook them since they will cook sufficiently with the turkey.

Veal Marsala—An Italian classic.

Four 5-ounce veal cutlets
¼ cup stone-ground whole-wheat flour
1 teaspoon salt
½ teaspoon ground black pepper
2 tablespoons olive oil
⅓ cup Marsala wine
2 tablespoons butter
2 tablespoons chopped fresh parsley

Pound the cutlets to a thickness of less than ⅛ inch with a meat tenderizer or mallet. Mix together the flour, salt, and pepper. Dredge the cutlets to coat in the mixture, shaking off excess flour. Preheat a large nonstick skillet over medium-high heat. Add the oil, then the cutlets. Cook for 1 minute, turn the cutlets over, and cook for 1 minute more. Add the wine and butter, and cook until the butter has melted, about 1 minute. Top the cutlets with the sauce from the pan and garnish with parsley.

Serves 4.

Note: Veal is an excellent source of B complex vitamins. It is also lean and low in fat.

Veal Piccata—Another winner.

Four 3-ounce veal cutlets
¼ cup stone-ground whole-wheat flour
½ teaspoon salt
¼ teaspoon ground black pepper
2 tablespoons olive oil
3 tablespoons dry white wine
2 tablespoons butter
2 tablespoons fresh lemon juice
2 teaspoons grated lemon zest (peel)
2 sprigs fresh parsley

Tenderize the cutlets by pounding them thin with a mallet or meat tenderizer. Mix together the flour, salt, and pepper on a plate and dredge the cutlets in the mixture, shaking off excess flour. Preheat a large nonstick skillet over medium heat. Add the oil, then the cutlets. Cook until lightly browned, about 1 minute a side. Remove the cutlets to a plate, and cover with aluminum foil to keep warm. Add the wine to the skillet and cook for about 30 seconds. Add the butter and lemon juice, and cook for about 1 minute more, until the butter has melted. Plate the cutlets, pour the sauce on top, sprinkle with lemon zest, and garnish with parsley sprigs.

Serves 2.

Note: Thin veal cutlets are sometimes labeled veal "scaloppine." For quick-cooking veal dishes such as this, the cutlets should be pounded to a thickness of less than ⅛ inch. Put them between sheets of wax paper or plastic wrap. If you don't have a meat tenderizer or mallet, you can use the side of a cleaver or the bottom of a flat skillet.

Veal Scaloppine with Tomatoes—A timeless favorite.

Four 5-ounce veal cutlets
¼ cup stone-ground whole-wheat flour
1 tablespoon olive oil
1 tablespoon butter
1 medium tomato, seeded and chopped
1 cup sliced white button mushrooms
½ cup dry white wine
½ teaspoon salt
¼ teaspoon ground black pepper

Using a metal mallet or a meat tenderizer, pound the cutlets to a thickness of less than ⅛ inch. Put the flour on a plate and dredge the cutlets in it, shaking off excess flour. Preheat a large nonstick skillet over medium heat. Add the oil and butter. When the butter has melted, add the cutlets, cook for 1 minute a side, and re-move to a plate. Add the tomatoes and mush-rooms to the skillet and cook, stirring constantly, until browned, 1 to 2 minutes. Add the wine and cook for 30 seconds to allow the alcohol to evaporate. Plate the cutlets, spoon the sauce on top, and sprinkle with salt and pepper.

Serves 4.

Note: Choose veal cutlets that are creamy white rather than dark pink; the lighter the meat, the more tender. The texture should be firm and smooth, not mushy.

Veal Chops—Young, tender beef.

1 teaspoon dried rosemary
½ teaspoon dried oregano
½ teaspoon ground black pepper
Four 8-ounce veal chops (about 1-inch-thick)
Light sprinkling of salt

Preheat the broiler. Mix together the rosemary, oregano, and pepper in a small bowl. Rub the mixture into both sides of the chops and sprinkle with salt. Broil about 5 minutes a side for medium doneness.

Serves 4.

Note: The chops can also be cooked in a dry (large nonstick) skillet for 6 minutes a side over medium heat. In addition to seasoning the chops with rosemary and oregano, we have also used a tarragon and thyme mixture, which produces a more pungent, distinctive flavor. See page 40 for a list of spices that go well with veal, and create your own customized veal chop. Be careful with such experimentation lest it becomes contagious, and you find yourself spending more and more enjoyable hours in the kitchen!

VII | Vegetables

Vegetables are primarily carbohydrates and carbohydrates are sugar in the broad sense. Your body gets most of its energy from sugar, so sugar from vegetables, fruits, or dairy products is required for you to survive and live a healthy life. Too much sugar, however, even from certain vegetables, can lead to problems for most people.

While your ancestors ate fruits and vegetables similar to what you eat today, they did not eat vegetables in a hybridized form. The hybridization of vegetables has been a fairly recent event in mankind's history. What does hybridization do for most vegetables? It makes them juicier, less fibrous or tough, tastier, and generally more pleasing in color. Unfortunately, some of these seemingly positive changes do present us with problems. One significant problem arises when the natural fiber is reduced, and the glycemic index or blood sugar stimulating effect increases. This is particularly true for white potatoes and corn, which now have a glycemic index exceeding that of table sugar.

Fortunately, there are only a few vegetables (and fruits) that fall in the high-glycemic category. As you can see from Table I beginning on page 4, the number of moderate to low-glycemic vegetables far outnumber the few that are high. This is what makes adhering to the SUGAR BUSTERS! lifestyle so easy.

We encourage you to eat a good variety of high-fiber, low-glycemic vegetables every day. From them you will get the sugar you need for energy and the fiber to benefit your digestive system. You will also get the balance you need to prevent you from becoming ketotic (in a state of acidosis), which can occur if you consistently eat mostly protein and fat. A tremendous number of vegetable recipes exist. We have simply included a variety in this cookbook to enable you to have some easy choices that can be prepared for a quick meal or that can augment a more leisurely gourmet dinner.

Vegetable Recipes

Steamed Artichokes, page 217

Instant Asparagus, page 219

Easy Avocado, page 220

Beans:

Black Beans, page 221

Garlic Green Beans, page 223

Simple Green Bean Casserole, page 224

Green Bean and Chestnut Casserole, page 225

Green Beans and Horseradish Sauce, page 227

Green Beans Italiano, page 229

Green Beans with Mustard Sauce, page 231

Kidney (red) Beans with Ham, page 233

Lentils, page 235

Spicy Lentils, page 236

Lima Beans, page 237

Lima Beans in Sour Cream, page 238

Pinto Beans, page 240

White Beans, page 241

Balsamic Broccoli, page 243

Cool Cabbage, page 244

Creamy Cabbage Slaw, page 245

Sour Cream Cole Slaw, page 246

Sweet and Sour Cabbage, page 247

Steamed Cauliflower, page 249

Smothered Eggplant, page 250

Stuffed Eggplant, page 251

Roasted Garlic, page 253

Smothered Greens, page 254

Turnip Greens, page 256

Sautéed Mushrooms, page 258

Okra and Tomatoes, page 259

Fried Okra, page 261

Smothered Okra, page 262

Spicy Okra and Tomatoes, page 263

Blackeyed Peas, page 264

Baked Sweet Potato, page 266

Brown Fried Rice, page 267

Curried Rice, page 269

Green Chili-Squash Casserole, page 270

Squash Casserole, page 272

Squash Con Queso, page 273

Creole Spinach, page 274

Sassy Spinach Stuffed Tomatoes, page 275

Sautéed Spinach, page 277

Spicy Spinach, page 279

Broiled Tomatoes, page 280

Fried Green Tomatoes, page 281

Marinated Vegetables, page 282

Sautéed Vegetables, page 283

Instant Zucchini, page 285

Smothered Zucchini, page 286

Steamed Artichokes—Leaves and all!

1 large artichoke
1 lemon wedge
2 cups water
½ cup olive oil
½ teaspoon garlic salt
1 tablespoon fresh lemon juice
3 large cloves garlic, finely chopped

Cut the stem of the artichoke flush with the base. If you choose, clip the sharp point at the end of each leaf with scissors. Cut in half lengthwise and remove the fuzzy chokes with a spoon or the tip of a knife. Rub the cut sides with the lemon wedge. Place in a medium saucepan and add the water. Bring to a boil. Cover, reduce the heat to medium-low to maintain a slow boil, and cook until the tip of a knife easily pierces the stem end and the large center leaves pull off readily, 25 to 30 minutes. In a small bowl, combine the oil, garlic salt, lemon juice, and garlic. Stir well to make a dip. Drain the artichoke, and serve with the dip on the side.

Serves 2.

Note: Artichokes are a good source of folate, magnesium, vitamin C, and dietary fiber, especially when you also eat a portion of the leaves. To eat an artichoke, just pull off individual leaves, dip them in the sauce, and scrape the tender meat from the bottom half of the leaf with your teeth. And don't forget the heart, which many consider the best part.

Vegetables

Instant Asparagus—Truly "instant."

1 pound fresh asparagus
1 tablespoon water
2 tablespoons no sugar added French dressing

Snap off the thick stem ends of the asparagus spears and rinse. Put the water in a microwave-safe container, add the asparagus, and cover with a paper towel. Microwave at full power until crisp tender, 2 to 4 minutes, depending upon the thickness of the spears and the wattage of your microwave. Add dressing and serve.

Serves 4.

Note: Only ½ cup provides 41 percent of the United States recommended daily allowance (U.S.RDA) for vitamin C. Asparagus is at its best in the spring; choose firm, brightly colored spears.

Easy Avocado—An easy vegetable to add at the last minute.

1 ripe avocado
¼ lemon
2 teaspoons no sugar added French dressing
Salt to taste

Cut the avocado in half lengthwise and remove the pit. Lay the halves cut side up on salad plates, squeeze lemon juice on top, and drizzle with French dressing. Sprinkle with salt.

Serves 2.

Note: Since the avocado halves are served in the skins, serve with spoons to scoop out the flesh. Don't hesitate to add a little more dressing, lemon juice, or salt to taste as you eat the avocado.

Vegetables

Black Beans—A dieter's delight.

1 pound dried black beans, rinsed and
   picked over
2 ½ quarts (10 cups) water
1 cup diced cooked ham (not sugar-cured)
1 large yellow onion, chopped
1 stalk celery, sliced
2 bay leaves
1 tablespoon Worcestershire sauce
1 teaspoon salt
½ teaspoon ground black pepper
Diced onions and tomatoes, to garnish
   (optional)
Homemade salsa (page 324), to garnish
   (optional)

Combine the beans, water, ham, onion, celery, and bay leaves in a Dutch oven. Bring to a very low boil over medium heat and cook for 1 hour, adjusting the heat as needed to maintain a simmer. Remove and discard the bay leaves. Add the Worcestershire sauce, salt, pepper, and more water if needed. Cover and maintain a simmer until the beans are slightly tender, 15 to 30 minutes. Serve with a sprinkling of diced onions and tomatoes, if desired, or with homemade salsa.

Serves 8 to 10.

Note: A high-fiber, high-protein carbohydrate. Black beans are ideal for someone attempting to lose weight because the beans are both filling and low-glycemic.

Garlic Green Beans—A 10-minute dish.

1 pound fresh green beans, ends snapped
2 teaspoons olive oil
½ teaspoon garlic salt

Rinse the beans, leaving a little water clinging to facilitate even steaming. Put them in a microwave-safe container and cover with plastic wrap. Microwave at full power until just crisp tender, 3 to 5 minutes, depending on the wattage of your microwave. Toss with the oil and garlic salt.

Serves 4 to 6.

Note: The beans will cook a bit faster if you snap them in half before microwaving. If you don't like garlic, substitute table salt.

Vegetables

Simple Green Bean Casserole—More easily prepared than most casseroles.

½ cup canola oil

1 medium white onion, sliced and separated into rings

One 9-ounce package frozen cut green beans, thawed, or one 14½-ounce can cut green beans, rinsed and drained

One 10¾-ounce can cream of mushroom soup

Preheat the oven to 350 degrees. Preheat a medium saucepan over high heat. Add the oil and heat until barely smoking, about 3 minutes. In batches, add onions and flash fry until browned, about 30 seconds. Remove the onions and drain on paper towels. Combine the green beans and soup in a 1-quart ovenproof casserole dish. Scatter the onions over the mixture and bake until golden brown on top, about 25 minutes.

Serves 4 to 6.

Note: So as not to spatter the very hot oil in which the onions are fried, use a pan with high, straight sides, such as a saucepan; don't crowd the pan, and retrieve the onions with a slotted spoon.

Green Bean and Chestnut Casserole—Worth the effort.

1 stick butter

Three 9-ounce packages frozen cut green beans, thawed, or three 14½-ounce cans cut green beans, rinsed and drained

1 medium yellow onion, diced

½ pound sliced white button mushrooms or two 4-ounce cans mushroom pieces, rinsed and drained

3 cups milk

¼ cup stone-ground whole-wheat flour

2 teaspoons soy sauce

1 teaspoon Worcestershire sauce

¼ teaspoon Tabasco or other hot sauce (or to taste)

1 teaspoon seasoned salt

1 teaspoon ground black pepper

1 teaspoon Accent (optional)

One 15-ounce can sliced water chestnuts, rinsed and drained

¼ cup natural sliced almonds

Preheat the oven to 300 degrees. Melt ½ stick of the butter in a medium nonstick skillet over medium-high heat. Add the beans, onion, and mushrooms. Sauté until the vegetables are soft, about 8 minutes. In a bowl, whisk together the milk, flour, soy sauce, Worcestershire sauce, hot sauce, seasoned salt, pepper, and Accent, if desired. Pour the mixture into the skillet, add the remaining ½ stick butter, and stir until well blended. Add the water chestnuts and almonds. Transfer to a 2-quart ovenproof casserole dish and bake until bubbly and lightly browned, about 30 minutes.

Serves 10 to 12.

Note: This dish is a meal in itself. Simply serve with a green salad. For a crispier topping, sprinkle the sliced almonds on top of the casserole rather than mixing them in.

Green Beans and Horseradish Sauce—A dish with some kick.

¼ pound diced cooked ham or bacon (not
　　sugar-cured)
1 large yellow onion, sliced
Two 9-ounce packages frozen cut green beans,
　　thawed, or two 14½-ounce cans cut green
　　beans, rinsed and drained
1 cup water
1 cup mayonnaise
2 hard-boiled eggs, chopped
1 heaping tablespoon prepared horseradish
1 teaspoon Worcestershire sauce
½ teaspoon garlic salt
½ teaspoon celery salt
½ teaspoon onion salt
Ground black pepper to taste
1 tablespoon chopped fresh parsley
Juice of 1 lemon

Combine the meat and onion in a large saucepan over medium-high heat. Stirring occasionally, cook until the meat is lightly browned and
the onion translucent, 2 to 3 minutes. Add the
beans and water. Cover, reduce the heat to low,
and simmer until the beans are tender, about

20 minutes. Meanwhile, combine the mayonnaise, eggs, horseradish, Worcestershire sauce, garlic salt, celery salt, onion salt, pepper, parsley, and lemon juice in a bowl. Mix well. Drain the bean mixture, put on a serving plate, and spoon the horseradish sauce on top.

Serves 8.

Note: These are excellent leftover and cold. If you like a very hot sauce on your beans, add up to 2 tablespoons of the prepared horseradish. If you use canned beans, choose a low-sodium brand or cut back a bit on one of the salts added to the dish.

Vegetables

Green Beans Italiano—Parmesan is always good on beans

⅓ cup olive oil

1 medium yellow onion, diced

1 medium green bell pepper, cored, seeded, and diced

1 clove garlic, peeled

Two 9-ounce packages frozen cut green beans, thawed, or two 14½-ounce cans cut green beans, rinsed and drained

1 teaspoon dried basil

Salt and ground black pepper to taste

⅓ cup grated Parmesan cheese

Preheat the oven to 350 degrees. Preheat a large skillet over high heat. Add the oil, then the onion and bell pepper. Press in the garlic. Stirring occasionally, cook until the onion is lightly browned, about 2 minutes. Stir in the beans and basil. Add salt and pepper to taste. Transfer to a 1-quart ovenproof casserole dish and sprinkle with Parmesan cheese. Bake until the cheese has browned, about 10 minutes.

Serves 5 or 6.

Note: In addition to oven baking, you could also cook the casserole in a microwave oven at full power for about 2½ minutes. Remember that Parmesan cheese is salty; don't add too much additional salt.

Vegetables

Green Beans with Mustard Sauce—Another good green bean dish.

2 egg yolks, beaten
1 teaspoon stone-ground whole-wheat flour
½ teaspoon dry mustard
¼ teaspoon salt
¾ cup scalded milk
Juice of ½ lemon
¾ pound fresh green beans, ends snapped, or
one 9-ounce package frozen cut green beans,
thawed

Whisk together the eggs, flour, dry mustard, and salt in the top of a double boiler over simmering water. Whisking constantly, slowly add the milk, and cook until the sauce is thickened enough to coat the back of a wooden spoon, about 4 minutes. Squeeze in the lemon juice and stir. Microwave fresh beans at full power until just crisp tender, 3 to 5 minutes, or cook frozen beans according to package directions. Transfer the beans to a serving plate and spoon the sauce on top.

Serves 4.

Note: Fresh or frozen green beans are an excellent source of fiber, vitamin A, and vitamin C. To scald milk, heat in a small saucepan over medium heat just until the milk begins to give off steam and bubbles form around the edge, 3 to 4 minutes.

Vegetables

Kidney (red) Beans with Ham—In New Orleans, these beans would be served with rice (brown, of course).

1 pound dried kidney beans, rinsed and
  picked over
2 quarts (8 cups) water
1½ cups diced cooked ham (not sugar-cured)
1 medium yellow onion, chopped
1 clove garlic, chopped
2 large bay leaves
Ground black pepper to taste
1 teaspoon salt

Combine the beans and water in a large saucepan. Bring to a boil over medium-high heat. Meanwhile, sauté the ham in a medium nonstick skillet over high heat until lightly browned, 4 to 5 minutes. Remove the meat to a bowl and add the onion and garlic to the skillet. Sauté until the onion is lightly browned, about 2 minutes. Add the ham, onion, garlic, bay leaves, and pepper to the beans. Bring back to a boil, cover, and reduce the heat to medium-low. Simmer until slightly tender, about 1 hour, adding more water if necessary. Remove and discard the bay leaves. Stir in the salt and serve.

Vegetables

Serves 8 to 10.

Note: Kidney beans are among the highest in fiber content of the bean family. Although we use red kidney beans in this recipe, you could easily substitute white kidney beans, also called cannellini beans.

Lentils—A good source of vegetable protein.

1 pound dried lentils, rinsed and picked over
1 quart (4 cups) water
½ cup olive oil
1 large yellow onion, finely chopped
Salt and ground black pepper to taste

Combine the lentils and water in a 3-quart saucepan and bring to a boil. Cover, reduce the heat to medium-low, and simmer until slightly tender, 15 to 20 minutes. Drain and set aside. In a medium skillet, warm the oil and sauté onion until the onion is translucent, about 4 minutes. Add the lentils, salt, and pepper. Cook for about 5 minutes more to heat through. Add more salt if needed.

Serves 8 to 10.

Note: Lentils have been around since biblical times, and were introduced to America by European and Asian immigrants. They supply a generous dose of dietary fiber and protein; in the Middle East, lentils have long been used as a meat substitute.

Spicy Lentils—RO•TEL tomatoes can spice up any dish.

1 pound dried lentils, rinsed and picked over
4 cups water
1 medium yellow onion, chopped
¼ cup extra virgin olive oil
One 10-ounce can RO•TEL diced tomatoes and
    chilies
2 teaspoons salt

Combine the lentils and water in a large saucepan. Bring to a simmer over medium heat. Cover, reduce the heat to medium-low, and simmer until slightly tender, about 15 minutes. In a small skillet, sauté the onion in the oil over high heat until limp, about 2 minutes. Add the onion and tomatoes to the lentils, stirring gently. Cook for 10 to 15 minutes to allow the flavors to blend. Add the salt.

Serves 4 to 6.

Note: Lentils are a tremendous source of folic acid. Just a ½ cup serving of lentils supplies almost 90 percent of the United States recommended daily allowance (U.S.RDA) for folic acid. Use red, brown, or green lentils in this dish.

Vegetables

Lima Beans—Better known as butter beans in the Deep South.

3 cups diced cooked ham (not sugar-cured)
1 large yellow onion, chopped
1 clove garlic, chopped
1 pound dried lima beans, rinsed and
   picked over
1½ quarts (6 cups) water
2 large bay leaves
Salt and ground black pepper to taste

Brown the ham in a 3-quart nonstick saucepan over medium-high heat, about 4 minutes. Add the onion and garlic, and sauté until the onion is translucent, about 3 minutes. Add the beans, stirring to coat. Add the water and bay leaves, and bring to a boil. Reduce the heat to medium-low and simmer until slightly tender, about 45 minutes. Remove and discard the bay leaves. Season with salt and pepper.

Serves 8 to 10.

Note: Lima beans were named for the capital city of Peru. Limas are unusually high in fiber, containing 6.9 grams per ½ cup serving. They are also a good source of vegetable protein.

Lima Beans in Sour Cream—A tasty way to prepare limas.

¾ pound dried lima beans, rinsed and
   picked over
3 quarts (12 cups) water
2 green onions or shallots (bulb only), finely
   chopped
½ cup finely chopped red pimiento
2 tablespoons olive or canola oil
½ cup reduced-fat sour cream
Salt and ground black pepper to taste

Combine the lima beans and water in a Dutch oven. Bring to a boil over high, then reduce the heat to medium and gently boil until slightly tender, about 1 hour. Meanwhile sauté the onion and pimiento in the oil in a medium nonstick skillet over medium-high heat until the onion has browned, about 3 minutes. Drain the beans and transfer to a large bowl. Stir in the onion, pimiento mixture, and the sour cream. Salt and pepper to taste.

Serves 8 or more.

Note: Limas, as with most beans, are very good leftover. You could use a green onion and a shallot instead of 2 onions of either variety in this dish. For a slightly spicier version, stir in a tablespoon of apple cider vinegar and a pinch of cayenne pepper just before serving.

Pinto Beans—The original ranch bean.

1 pound dried pinto beans, rinsed and
   picked over
3 quarts (12 cups) water
2 large yellow onions, peeled and chopped
3 slices bacon, chopped
Salt and ground black pepper to taste

Combine the beans and water in a 3-quart saucepan. Bring to a boil and maintain at a simmer
over medium heat for about 1 hour, checking
periodically to see if more water is needed. Add
the onion and bacon, and continue to cook until
tender, 30 to 60 minutes. Add salt and pepper to
taste.

Serves 4 to 6.

Note: Salsa (see page 324) is a great enhance-
ment for either pinto or black beans. This is
true whether you serve the beans on the plate or
as a quasi soup in a bowl with a lot of the cooking liquid left with the beans. Pintos are a particularly strong source of folic acid, containing
over 70 percent of the U.S.RDA in a ½ cup serving. You can replace the bacon in this recipe
with 2 tablespoons bacon drippings.

Vegetables

White Beans—Also known as Great Northern or navy beans.

1 pound Great Northern beans, rinsed and
    picked over
2 quarts (8 cups) water
1 tablespoon olive oil
1 cup diced cooked ham (not sugar-cured)
1 medium yellow onion, chopped
1 clove garlic, chopped
½ teaspoon dried rosemary
Salt and ground black pepper to taste

Combine the beans and water in a 3-quart sauce-pan. Bring to a boil over high heat. Meanwhile, combine the oil, ham, onion, and garlic in a medium nonstick skillet. Sauté over medium-high heat until the meat has browned, 4 to 5 minutes. Add the contents of the skillet to the beans, along with the rosemary, and reduce the heat to medium-low. Continue to cook until the beans are slightly tender, about 1 hour, adding more water if necessary. Season with salt and pepper.

Serves 8 to 10.

Note: Great Northerns supply almost 20 percent of your daily iron requirement. You can season all varieties of dried beans with fresh herbs. Choose herbs that complement the dishes that will go with the beans; see pages 38 to 47 for recommendations on how to season various foods.

Vegetables

Balsamic Broccoli—Very nutritious.

½ cup water
1 teaspoon salt
3 large stalks broccoli, cut into 1-inch florets
1 tablespoon olive oil
4 cloves garlic, peeled and crushed
1 small jalapeño pepper, cored, seeded,
    deveined, and minced
¼ cup balsamic vinegar

Bring the water to a boil in a 3-quart saucepan. Add the salt and broccoli. Bring back to a boil and boil until the broccoli is crisp tender, about 3 minutes. Drain and set aside. Meanwhile, combine the oil, garlic, and jalapeño pepper in a medium skillet over medium heat. Sauté until the garlic has just begun to brown, 1 to 2 minutes. Add the broccoli and vinegar, reduce the heat to medium-low, and cook for 2 minutes.

Serves 4.

Note: Look for broccoli with tight, bright purple-green florets; the appearance of little yellow flowers indicates broccoli is past its prime and might be bitter. You can get 100 percent of your U.S.RDA for vitamin C and 10 percent of vitamin A by eating just a ½ cup of cooked broccoli.

Cool Cabbage—This recipe is particularly good.

1 red or sweet onion, chilled
4 cups finely shredded green cabbage, chilled
½ cup chopped flat-leaf parsley
3 tablespoons canola oil
¼ cup apple cider vinegar
2 packets artificial sweetener
1 teaspoon salt

Quarter the onion lengthwise, then cut each quarter crosswise into 1-inch-long pieces. Combine the onion, cabbage, and parsley in a large bowl. In a small bowl, mix together the oil, vinegar, artificial sweetener, and salt. Pour the dressing over the vegetables and toss well.

Serves 4.

Note: Cabbage is a member of the mustard family. This cabbage slaw is ready with no chilling needed, since the ingredients are chilled before you start.

Creamy Cabbage Slaw—A more conventional slaw.

3 cups shredded green or red cabbage
1 bunch green onions, trimmed and sliced
1 large stalk celery, sliced
½ cup mayonnaise
1 tablespoon white vinegar
½ teaspoon salt
1 packet artificial sweetener (optional)

Combine the cabbage, green onions, and celery in a large bowl. In a small bowl whisk together the mayonnaise, vinegar, salt, and artificial sweetener, if desired. Add the dressing to the slaw and toss to coat. Cover and chill for 15 minutes in the freezer or 1 hour in the refrigerator.

Serves 4.

Note: Both red and green cabbage are rich in vitamin C and vitamin A.

Sour Cream Cole Slaw—One more version of slaw.

½ cup reduced-fat sour cream
2 tablespoons apple cider vinegar
3 packets artificial sweetener
½ teaspoon salt
⅛ teaspoon ground black pepper (or to taste)
½ head green cabbage, finely shredded

In a small bowl, combine the sour cream, vinegar, artificial sweetener, salt, and pepper. Stir to blend. Put the cabbage into a large bowl, add the dressing, and toss to coat. Chill in the freezer for 10 to 15 minutes.

Serves 4.

Note: Look for cabbages with firm-looking leaves that are tightly packed.

Vegetables

Sweet and Sour Cabbage—Red cabbage and cloves make this special.

8 slices bacon, diced
1 medium red onion, finely chopped
4 cups finely shredded red cabbage
4 whole cloves
¼ teaspoon salt plus additional to taste
¼ teaspoon ground black pepper plus
    additional to taste
⅓ cup plus 2 tablespoons balsamic vinegar
½ cup water

In a large skillet, fry the bacon until crisp over medium heat, 6 to 8 minutes. Remove the bacon to paper towels to drain. Add the onion to the skillet. Stirring constantly, cook until translucent, about 3 minutes. Add the cabbage, cloves, salt, and pepper. Still stirring, cook for 3 minutes to coat the cabbage. Add the vinegar and water. Cover, reduce the heat to low, and simmer until the cabbage is tender, about 7 minutes. Uncover, raise the heat to high, and boil off any excess liquid. Crumble the bacon into the cabbage, and add more salt and pepper to taste.

Serves 4.

Note: Red cabbage is even higher in vitamin C than common cabbage, supplying over 40 percent of the U.S.RDA in a ½ cup serving. If you don't have any whole cloves on hand, use ⅛ teaspoon ground cloves. For added texture, sweetness, and color, toss a diced Granny Smith apple into the cabbage when you add the bacon.

Steamed Cauliflower—A good source of vitamin C.

1 large head cauliflower
½ cup water
⅛ teaspoon salt

Break the cauliflower into bite-size pieces and put it into a large nonstick skillet. Add the water and salt. Bring to a slow boil over medium-high heat and cook until the cauliflower is slightly tender, 5 to 7 minutes. Drain and serve. If desired, sprinkle with cheese or with about ½ teaspoon of the seasoning of your choice, such as Season•All, Tony Cachere's, or Lawry's salt.

Serves 4 to 6.

Note: For optimum nutrition and to achieve the lowest blood sugar stimulating (glycemic) result, vegetables like cauliflower should be eaten raw. The flavor of raw vegetables still can be enhanced by a sprinkling of the previously mentioned seasonings.

Smothered Eggplant—Filling but not fattening.

2 small or 1 medium eggplant, peeled and
  cubed
Warm water
1 teaspoon salt plus additional to taste
½ cup canola oil
1 medium yellow onion, chopped
1 medium green bell pepper, cored, seeded, and
  chopped
Ground black pepper to taste

Put the eggplant into a large bowl, cover with warm water, add the 1 teaspoon salt, and let soak for 20 minutes. Drain and set aside. Preheat a large skillet over medium heat. Add the oil, then the eggplant, onion, bell pepper, salt, and black pepper. Cover, reduce the heat to medium-low, and cook until tender, 5 to 7 minutes.

Serves 6 to 8.

Note: Although native to India, eggplants are believed to have been introduced into America by Thomas Jefferson, who was an ardent gardener. For a colorful addition to this dish, stir in a chopped fresh tomato or one 14½-ounce can diced tomatoes along with the onion and bell pepper.

Stuffed Eggplant—A one dish meal.

5 cups water
2 medium eggplants
3 tablespoons olive oil
1 small yellow onion, chopped
2 tablespoons chopped shallot (bulb only)
1 pound cooked and peeled medium shrimp
½ pound lump crabmeat, cartilage and shells
    removed
2 tablespoons chopped fresh parsley
1 large egg, beaten
Juice of 1 lemon
1 tablespoon Worcestershire sauce
Salt and ground black pepper to taste
½ cup grated Parmesan cheese

Preheat the oven to 375 degrees. Bring 4 cups of
the water to a boil in a 3-quart saucepan. Cut the
eggplant in half lengthwise. Scoop out the pulp
leaving only ¼ inch of the meat intact and reserving the shells. Add the pulp to the boiling
water, reduce the heat to medium-low, and simmer for 5 minutes. Drain and set aside. Preheat a
medium skillet over medium-high heat. Add the
oil, then the onion and shallot. Sauté until soft,
2 to 3 minutes. Add the eggplant pulp, shrimp,

crabmeat, and parsley, then the egg, lemon juice, Worcestershire sauce, salt, and pepper. Mix well. Spoon the mixture into the reserved eggplant shells. Place the shells into a 7-by-12-inch baking dish, add the remaining 1 cup water to the dish, and sprinkle with the Parmesan cheese. Bake until browned, about 25 minutes.

Serves 4.

Note: This dish contains everything you need for a complete meal if simply accompanied by a green salad.

Vegetables

Roasted Garlic—For the true garlic lovers.

1 head garlic (unpeeled)
2 tablespoons olive oil
1 teaspoon chopped fresh rosemary
¼ teaspoon salt
2 slices stone-ground whole-wheat bread

Preheat the oven to 400 degrees. Slice off the top of the garlic bulb, exposing the cloves. Place in a small ovenproof dish. Pour 1 tablespoon of the oil on top. Roast for 20 minutes. Remove the dish from the oven and preheat the broiler. Separate the garlic cloves, put them back into the dish, add the remaining 1 tablespoon oil, and sprinkle with the rosemary and salt. Broil until crisp and well browned on top, about 5 minutes. Coat the bread with the roasting liquid or a little plain olive oil, toast lightly, and spread the roasted garlic on top.

Serves 2 to 6, depending upon your love of garlic!

Note: Garlic has been said to be a natural blood thinner and has been used for centuries as a "cure" for various maladies. Make sure to broil the garlic in a dish that will withstand the intense heat of a broiler.

Smothered Greens—Come get your beta-carotene.

2 bunches mustard greens
1 gallon (16 cups) water
4 slices bacon, chopped
½ cup olive oil
¼ cup stone-ground whole-wheat flour
1 medium green bell pepper, cored, seeded, and chopped
1 medium yellow onion, chopped
Salt and ground black pepper to taste

Wash the greens and soak the leaves in a large pot of warm salted water for 10 minutes. Put the 1 gallon of water into a stockpot and bring to a boil over high heat. Add the greens and boil for 15 minutes, then drain. In a large skillet over medium heat, cook the bacon until just beginning to color. Add the oil and flour, and continue to cook, stirring constantly, until the mixture becomes golden brown, 3 to 5 minutes. Add the greens, bell pepper, onion, salt, and black pepper. Cover, reduce the heat to medium-low, and cook until very tender, about 25 minutes.

Serves 4 to 6.

Note: Mustard greens contain 30, 26, and 21 percent, respectively, of the United States' recommended daily allowance for vitamin C, folic acid, and vitamin A.

Turnip Greens—Full of antioxidants and fiber.

½ pound fresh turnip greens or two 10-ounce
   packages frozen whole turnip greens
1 quart (4 cups) water
2 slices bacon chopped
1 small yellow onion, minced
Salt and ground black pepper to taste

If using frozen greens, put in a microwave-safe
container and microwave at full power for about
4 minutes to thaw. In a 3-quart saucepan, bring
the water to a boil. Add the greens and boil for
5 minutes. Drain, squeeze out excess water, and
set aside. Put the bacon and onion in a large
skillet. Stirring constantly, cook over medium-
low heat until the onion turns translucent and
the bacon is slightly crisp, about 6 minutes. Add
the greens. Still stirring, cook for about 5 minutes more, until tender and wilted. Salt and pepper to taste.

Serves 4.

Note: Turnip greens are very nutritious, supplying 40 percent of the United States recommended daily allowance for vitamin A and 33
percent of vitamin C, two of the three key

antioxidants. Two 14½-ounce cans chicken broth can be substituted for the water. If you cook the greens in chicken broth, do not drain. Add the contents of the skillet to the saucepan with the greens, bring to a boil, and boil for 1 minute. Serve the greens in small bowls, along with the cooking liquid.

Sautéed Mushrooms—Another dieter's delight.

One 8-ounce package white button
    mushrooms, trimmed
¼ cup olive oil
1 tablespoon balsamic vinegar (with no more
    than 1 gram of sugar per serving)
2 tablespoons chopped fresh parsley
Salt and ground black pepper to taste

Combine the mushrooms, oil, and vinegar in a large skillet over medium heat. Cook until tender, about 12 minutes, turning midway through. Add the parsley, salt, and pepper and cook for 10 seconds.

Serves 2 to 4.

Note: Mushrooms can be substituted for many roasted or broiled meats to make a vegetarian meal. Any combination of mushrooms can be used in place of plain white mushrooms, including portobellos, shiitakes, oysters, or creminis.

Vegetables

Okra and Tomatoes—A well-matched pair.

½ tablespoon salt
½ pound tender fresh okra, rinsed and drained
¼ cup canola oil
1 medium yellow onion, chopped
1 medium green bell pepper, cored, seeded, and
  chopped
2 slices bacon, chopped
One 14½-ounce can diced tomatoes, drained
2 packets artificial sweetener (optional)
½ teaspoon ground black pepper

Bring a medium saucepan of water to a boil over high heat. Add 1 teaspoon of the salt and the okra, and boil until tender, 8 to 10 minutes, then drain. As soon as the okra cools enough to handle, remove the stems and cut into chunks. In a large skillet, heat the oil over medium-high heat for about 2 minutes, then add the onion, bell pepper, and bacon. Sauté until the onion is lightly browned, about 2 minutes. Add the tomatoes, reduce the heat to medium-low, and cook 5 minutes. Add the okra, artificial sweetener, if desired, black pepper, and the remaining ½ teaspoon salt. Cook for 5 minutes more to heat through.

Serves 4 to 6.

Note: There is plenty of vitamin C in this dish as tomatoes supply nearly 40 percent and okra over 20 percent of the U.S.RDA. Look for tender okra pods—small young pods that are blemish free.

Fried Okra—For those who like okra crispy.

1 pound tender fresh okra
½ cup stone-ground whole-wheat flour
½ teaspoon salt
¼ teaspoon ground black pepper
1 cup canola or olive oil

Rinse, drain, and cut the okra into ½-inch pieces. Mix together the flour, salt, and pepper in a bowl, and toss the okra in the mixture to coat. Preheat the oil in a small saucepan. Add the okra, in batches, and fry until crisp, about 1 minute. Remove with a slotted spoon and drain on paper towels.

Serves 4.

Note: Use a heavy, high-sided pan, such as a saucepan, to prevent the hot oil from spattering. Test to see if your oil is hot enough by putting a single pod into the pan; if the oil sizzles, you're set to fry. If you use olive oil, which burns at a lower temperature than canola oil, take care not to let it smoke.

Vegetables

Smothered Okra—An old plantation staple.

3 tablespoons olive oil

2 pounds tender fresh okra, rinsed, drained, and cut into ½-inch pieces

1 medium white onion, chopped

1 medium green bell pepper, cored, seeded, and chopped

4 medium tomatoes, diced, or two 14½-ounce cans diced tomatoes

Salt and ground black pepper to taste

Preheat a large skillet over high heat. Add the oil and heat just until beginning to simmer, about 30 seconds. Add the okra, onion, and bell pepper. Sauté until the onion turns translucent, 2 to 3 minutes. Add the tomatoes. Cover, reduce the heat to medium, and cook until the okra is tender, 7 to 10 minutes, stirring occasionally. Season with salt and black pepper.

Serves 4 to 6.

Note: The Angolan word for okra is "ngombo," which explains the name for the popular Creole stew that features okra.

Vegetables

Spicy Okra and Tomatoes—A new twist to a traditional dish.

One 1-pound bag frozen cut okra
2 tablespoons canola oil
2 medium yellow onions, chopped
1 medium green bell pepper, cored, seeded, and
  minced
1 clove garlic, minced
One 10-ounce can RO•TEL diced tomatoes and
  chilies
One 8-ounce can tomato sauce
Salt and ground black pepper to taste

Cook the okra according to package directions, then rinse under cold running water to stop the cooking, and drain. Preheat a large skillet over medium-high heat. Add the oil, then the onions, bell pepper, and garlic. Sauté until the onions turn translucent, about 3 minutes. Add the okra, tomatoes, tomato sauce, salt, and black pepper. Cover, reduce the heat to medium-low, and simmer to heat through, 4 to 5 minutes.

Serves 6 to 8.

Note: RO•TEL tomatoes add some heat to every recipe in which they are used.

Blackeyed Peas—Don't wait until New Year's Day for this one.

3 quarts (12 cups) water
1 pound dried or frozen blackeyed peas
1 cup cubed cooked ham (not sugar-cured)
1 medium yellow onion, chopped
2 large stalks celery, chopped
2 cloves garlic, peeled
2 bay leaves
½ teaspoon dried oregano
½ teaspoon dried basil
½ teaspoon ground black pepper
3 dashes Tabasco or other hot sauce (or more to
    taste)
Salt to taste

Pour the water into a Dutch oven. Add the peas, ham, onion, celery, garlic, bay leaves, oregano, basil, and pepper. Bring to a boil over high heat. Reduce the heat to medium, and simmer, uncovered, for about 2 hours, until the peas are tender. Drain excess liquid, if any. Remove and discard the bay leaves, stir in the hot sauce, and salt to taste.

Serves 8.

Note: If frozen peas are used, thaw before beginning this recipe. For "instant" blackeyed peas, substitute 2 cans of cooked peas; eliminate the water and bay leaves from the recipe above, and cook, covered, for 30 minutes.

Baked Sweet Potato—Simple but simply nutritious.

1 small sweet potato, scrubbed
1 tablespoon butter, at room temperature
Light sprinkle of salt

Jab the sweet potato a few times with the tines of a fork. Wrap in a paper towel and cook in a microwave oven at full power until soft, 4 to 5 minutes. Remove to a plate, cut open lengthwise, add the butter and salt, and enjoy while still hot.

Serves 1.

Note: Sweet potatoes are extremely nutritious and provide a great source of beta-carotene. They can be kept in a bowl at room temperature for days, and then cooked very quickly when a vegetable is needed with many of your meat dishes. For variety, you can add a sprinkling of cinnamon, nutmeg, or even freshly ground black pepper.

Brown Fried Rice—Hey, it is still good!

2 tablespoons peanut oil
¼ pound sliced white button mushrooms or
   one 4-ounce can sliced mushrooms, rinsed
   and drained
2½ cups cooked brown rice
2 tablespoons soy sauce
1 large egg, beaten
6 slices bacon, crisp cooked and finely
   crumbled
2 green onions, trimmed and finely chopped

Preheat a large nonstick skillet over high heat.
Add the oil, then the mushrooms. Stir-fry until
limp, about 1 minute. Add the rice and soy
sauce and stir-fry until the grains of rice have
separated and coated, about 30 seconds. Push
the mushrooms and rice to the side of the pan
with a wooden spoon or paddle. Add the egg and
scramble for 30 seconds. Stir to break up the
rice, and mix the contents of the pan together.
Stir in the bacon and green onions, and stir-fry
for 30 seconds to 1 minute more to heat through.

Serves 4.

Note: Finely chopped, cooked pork, ham, or shrimp can be substituted for bacon. The key to stir-frying is to make sure that the pan is very hot before you start and to keep the food moving quickly, using a wooden spoon or paddle or two. Use leftover brown rice if you have any on hand; it will reheat nicely as you stir-fry.

Curried Rice—An East Indian staple (if brown rice counts!)

3 tablespoons butter
½ cup finely chopped white onion
1 clove garlic, finely minced
2 teaspoons curry powder
1 cup brown basmati rice
1 bay leaf
1¾ cups fresh or canned chicken broth

Melt 2 tablespoons of the butter in a medium saucepan over medium heat. Add the onion and garlic. Stirring constantly, cook until the onion is wilted, about 2 minutes. Stir in the curry powder and rice. Add the bay leaf and broth. Cover, reduce the heat to low, and cook until the rice is tender, 25 to 30 minutes. Stir in the remaining 1 tablespoon butter, fluff the rice, and serve.

Serves 4 to 6.

Note: Serve this with curried lamb and you may think you are in India! Brown rice contains 8½ times more fiber than white rice.

Green Chili-Squash Casserole—Another winner.

1 large stockpot of water
1 large butternut squash, quartered
1 teaspoon salt plus additional to taste
1 medium yellow onion, thinly sliced
One 4-ounce can chopped green chilies
½ cup whole-wheat cracker crumbs
2 cups grated sharp cheddar cheese
3 large eggs, beaten
1 cup low-fat milk
1 tablespoon Worcestershire sauce
Ground black pepper to taste

Preheat the oven to 400 degrees. Bring a large stockpot of water to a boil over high heat. Add the squash and 1 teaspoon salt and boil until fork tender in the center, about 20 minutes. Drain, peel the squash, and cut into slices less than ¼-inch-thick. In a large bowl, mix together the onion, chilies, cracker crumbs, cheese, eggs, milk, Worcestershire sauce, salt, and pepper. Fold in the squash. Scrape into a 3-quart ovenproof casserole dish, cover, and bake for 15 minutes. Remove the cover and bake for about 10 minutes more, until browned on top.

Serves 6.

Note: Fiber-rich butternut squash contains 71 percent of the recommended daily allowance for vitamin A and 26 percent of the recommended daily allowance for vitamin C.

Squash Casserole—Another good old standby.

6 yellow summer squash, diced
1 large yellow onion, sliced
1 cup shredded sharp cheddar cheese
One 8-ounce can tomato sauce
¼ teaspoon seasoned salt
2 packets artificial sweetener (optional)

Preheat the oven to 350 degrees. Combine the squash and onion in a microwave-safe container, cover, and microwave at full power until the squash is fork tender, about 4 minutes, or steam over simmering water. Transfer the vegetables to a 2-quart ovenproof casserole dish. Mix in the cheese, tomato sauce, seasoned salt, and artificial sweetener, if desired. Cover and bake for 20 minutes.

Serves 10 to 12.

Note: Yellow summer squash is sometimes labeled crookneck squash. You can easily substitute zucchini.

Squash Con Queso—Velveeta cheese makes this extra smooth.

2 tablespoons olive oil

6 yellow summer squash, cut into ¼-inch-
thick slices

1 medium yellow onion

1 cup coarsely grated Velveeta cheese

Salt and ground black pepper to taste

Chopped fresh chives or parsley, to garnish
(optional)

Preheat a large skillet over medium heat. Add
the oil and heat for 30 seconds. Add the squash
and onion and cook, stirring occasionally, until
the squash is crisp tender, 4 to 5 minutes. Stir in
the cheese and cook, stirring constantly, until it
has melted slightly, 1 to 2 minutes. Remove the
pan from the heat, season with salt and pepper,
and garnish with chopped chives or parsley, if
desired.

Serves 6 to 8.

Note: A uniquely American food, summer
crookneck squash is believed to be the first food
cultivated in America.

Creole Spinach—Come on vitamin A!

Two 10-ounce packages chopped frozen
   spinach
¾ stick butter
1 medium yellow onion, chopped
2 cloves garlic, chopped
Salt and ground black pepper to taste
3 tablespoons stone-ground whole-wheat flour
1⅓ cups low-fat milk
2 cups coarsely grated Velveeta cheese

Preheat the oven to 325 degrees. Cook the spinach according to package directions, drain, and squeeze out excess water. Melt the butter in a medium skillet over medium heat. Add the onion, garlic, salt, and pepper. Stirring constantly, cook until the onion softens a bit, about 3 minutes, then add the spinach. In a small bowl, dissolve the flour in the milk. Add to the skillet. Stir in the cheese. Scrape into a 1-quart ovenproof casserole dish and bake until lightly browned on top, about 25 minutes.

Serves 6 to 8.

Note: Still good the next day! Spinach supplies almost 75 percent of the U.S.RDA for vitamin A plus 66 percent of folic acid, 32 percent of iron, and 22 percent of magnesium in only ½ cup of cooked spinach.

Sassy Spinach Stuffed Tomatoes—Here comes that nutritious spinach again! And a holiday delight.

Four 10-ounce packages frozen whole leaf spinach
8 medium tomatoes
One 8-ounce jar Jalapeño Cheez Whiz
1 teaspoon onion powder
¾ teaspoon garlic powder
⅛ teaspoon salt
¼ teaspoon ground black pepper
8 pats butter

Preheat the oven to 350 degrees. Cook the spinach according to package directions. Meanwhile, slice ¼ inch off the top of each tomato. With a spoon, scoop out the inside pulp, taking care to remove the seeds and leaving the meat attached to the outer skin intact. Squeeze excess water from the spinach and put it in a large bowl. Stir in the Cheez Whiz. Add the onion powder, garlic powder, salt, and pepper. Mix well. Divide the mixture among the tomato shells. Top each with a pat of butter. Place the stuffed tomatoes in a baking dish and add just enough water to cover the bottom. Bake for about 10 minutes.

Serves 8.

Note: You can whip this up in minutes from ingredients you probably already have on hand. It's yet another way to savor nutritious spinach, here combined with tangy cheese and seasonings and stuffed into tomato shells.

Sautéed Spinach—If you don't like plain spinach, this one's for you.

2 strips bacon

2 tablespoons olive oil

¼ pound fresh sliced white button mushrooms or one 4-ounce can sliced mushrooms, rinsed and drained

One 10-ounce package fresh salad spinach, rinsed, drained, and torn

2 green onions, chopped (including some of the green tops)

Salt and ground black pepper to taste

In a large skillet over medium-low heat, cook the bacon until crisp, 6 to 8 minutes. Remove the bacon to paper towels to drain, leaving the drippings in the pan. Add the oil to the bacon drippings. Add the mushrooms and sauté over medium-high heat until tender, about 3 minutes. Add the spinach and green onions, reduce the heat to medium-low, and cook, stirring constantly, until wilted, 3 to 4 minutes. Season with salt and pepper. Crumble the bacon into the spinach and serve while still warm.

Serves 3 to 4.

Note: You can choose spinach labeled "salad" spinach when you buy this nutritional power-house. Salad spinach is triple washed and stemmed, requiring a quick rinse at most.

Vegetables

Spicy Spinach—Horseradish adds a kick to anything.

Two 10-ounce packages frozen chopped
   spinach
¼ cup low-fat milk
2 tablespoons butter
2 tablespoons prepared horseradish
½ teaspoon salt

Cook the spinach according to package directions, drain, and squeeze out excess water. Combine the milk, butter, horseradish, and salt in a small skillet. Stirring frequently, cook over medium-high heat until the butter has melted and the mixture is blended and slightly creamy, about 4 minutes. Stir in the spinach and cook for about 1 minute more to heat through and coat.

Serves 4 to 6.

Note: Nutritious spinach, a serving of which provides most of your recommended daily allowance for vitamin A, holds up remarkably well to the freezing process. Once cooked, there is very little difference in the taste or texture of fresh and frozen spinach.

Vegetables

Broiled Tomatoes—Tasty bites of Italian delights.

12 cherry tomatoes, halved lengthwise
½ tablespoon olive oil
2 cloves garlic, minced
2 tablespoons grated Parmesan cheese
1 teaspoon dried thyme
¼ teaspoon salt

Preheat the broiler. Toss the tomatoes in the oil in a bowl, then lay them on a broiler tray cut side up. In a small bowl, mix together the garlic, Parmesan cheese, thyme, and salt. Sprinkle the tomatoes with the mixture. Position about 4 inches from the heat source and broil until lightly browned and crusty, 1 to 1½ minutes.

Serves 4.

Note: Tomatoes contain almost 40 percent of the U.S.RDA for vitamin C. In this recipe, take care not to leave the tomatoes under the broiler for much more than 1½ minutes, or they will become mushy.

Fried Green Tomatoes—A great way to use green tomatoes.

½ cup stone-ground whole-wheat flour
½ cup grated Parmesan cheese
¼ teaspoon cayenne pepper
¼ teaspoon ground black pepper
⅛ teaspoon salt
1 cup buttermilk
1 cup canola or olive oil
2 medium green tomatoes, sliced

Mix together the flour, cheese, cayenne pepper, black pepper, and salt on a plate. Pour the buttermilk into a large, shallow bowl. Heat the oil over medium-high heat in a large, heavy skillet. Dip the tomato slices into the buttermilk and then dredge in the flour to coat, shaking off excess flour. Fry in the oil, in batches, until crisp and golden brown, 1 to 2 minutes per side.

Serves 4.

Note: Green tomatoes, which are tomatoes that have not yet ripened, are especially plentiful in the summer and fall. They are very firm, so they will hold their consistency when fried, and are less sweet than ripe red tomatoes.

*Marinated Vegetables—Raw vegetables are
the healthiest choice.*

2 cups of any combination of:
   Cauliflower, cut into florets
   Broccoli, cut into florets
   Celery stalks, sliced
   Any color bell pepper, cored, seeded, and cut
     into thin strips
   Vidalia, 1015, Walla Walla, or other sweet
     onion, sliced
   Yellow summer squash or zucchini, sliced
   Cucumber, sliced
   White button or baby portobello mushrooms,
     sliced
   Ripe tomatoes, cut into wedges, or cherry
     tomatoes, halved
1 cup Wish-Bone or other Italian salad dressing

Place all vegetables except tomatoes in a plastic storage bag. Add the dressing, press out excess air, seal tightly, and marinate for at least 12 hours in the refrigerator, turning once. If you wish to include tomatoes, add them to the bag and marinate for 1 hour. Drain and serve.

Serves 4 to 6.

Note: Because you are serving them raw, be sure to use tender, young vegetables that are blemish free, thoroughly rinsed, and trimmed.

Vegetables

Sautéed Vegetables—One healthy, nonfattening bite after another.

½ cup olive or canola oil
2 cups of any combination of:
　Broccoli, cut into florets
　Green or red cabbage, shredded
　Cauliflower, cut into florets
　Peeled and cubed eggplant
　Any color onion, sliced
　White button, portobello, oyster, or shiitake
　　mushrooms, sliced
　Any color bell pepper, cored, seeded, and cut
　　into thin strips
　Yellow summer squash or zucchini, cubed or
　　sliced
　Ripe tomatoes, cut into wedges
3 cloves garlic, chopped (optional)
Garlic salt or salt to taste
2 tablespoons chopped fresh flat-leaf parsley
1 or 2 teaspoons low-sugar balsamic vinegar
　(1 gram sugar)
½ lemon

Heat the oil in a large skillet over medium heat. Add the vegetables of your choice, the garlic, if desired, and the garlic salt or salt. Stirring constantly, cook until vegetables turn limp, tender, or translucent, 5 to 8 minutes. Stir in the parsley and vinegar. Cook and stir for 1 to 2 minutes more. If desired, squeeze lemon juice over the vegetables just before serving.

Serves 4.

Note: This is the authors' favorite cooked vegetable dish. It is quick and easy to cook and once mastered really requires no measuring of quantities. The resulting flavors, while varying somewhat, will always be tasty and also nutritious.

Vegetables

Instant Zucchini—Easy enough?

1 tablespoon butter
½ cup sliced yellow onion
2 zucchini, thinly sliced
1 tablespoon water
½ teaspoon salt
¼ teaspoon ground black pepper
2 tablespoons grated Parmesan cheese

Preheat a medium skillet over medium-high heat. Add the butter and let it melt. Add the onion and sauté until translucent, 2 to 3 minutes. Add the zucchini and water. Reduce the heat to medium-low and cook until crisp tender, about 4 minutes. Season with salt and pepper. Transfer to a serving dish and sprinkle with the Parmesan cheese.

Serves 4.

Note: If you are still stuck on calories, there are less than 15 calories in a ½ cup serving of boiled zucchini.

Vegetables

Smothered Zucchini—Zucchini with some Italian seasonings.

¼ cup butter
½ cup sliced yellow onion
¼ cup chopped green bell pepper
1 clove garlic, minced
½ teaspoon dried oregano
4 zucchini, thinly sliced
One 10¾-ounce can tomato soup
Salt and ground black pepper to taste
¼ cup grated Parmesan cheese

Melt the butter in a large skillet over medium-high heat. Add the onion, bell pepper, garlic, and oregano. Sauté until the onion is translucent, 2 to 3 minutes. Stir in the zucchini and soup. Reduce the heat to low and cook, stirring constantly, until the zucchini is crisp tender and the soup somewhat reduced, 4 to 5 minutes. Salt and pepper, and sprinkle with the Parmesan cheese before serving.

Serves 8.

Note: Fresh zucchini is available year-round, allowing you to enjoy this dish whenever you want. Choose bright colored young zucchini that are free of spots and firm to the touch.

VIII | Appetizers and Hors d'oeuvres

At home, as well as in many restaurants, the appetizers and hors d'oeuvres are the most highly flavored items on the menu. While getting you off to a mouthwatering start, such spicy dishes often overpower the more subtle flavors of your entrée and accompanying vegetables. So keep that in mind as you mix and match your meals so as not to be disappointed with your main dish.

A tip on eating out where the restaurant has a particularly splendid array of appetizers is to simply order two or three appetizers, interrupted by a good green salad to cleanse your palate, instead of ordering a main course. You can also do this at home for yourself or you can even surprise your guests with such a treat. Should you decide to try this, just remember to serve the appetizers or hors d'oeuvres in the order of ascending spiciness so the last one consumed will still be very flavorful to the taste buds.

Appetizers and Hors d'oeuvres Recipes

Bloody Mary Concentrate, page 290

Ceviche, page 291

Con Queso Dip, page 293

Crab Dip, page 294

Curry Vegetable Dip, page 295

Deviled Eggs, page 296

Oyster Ramakis, page 297

Oysters Tony, page 298

Mock Oysters, page 300

Spicy Oysters, page 301

Cherry Tomatoes and Prosciutto, page 302

Tuna and Cheese Spread, page 303

Bloody Mary Concentrate—Very handy to have on hand.

⅓ cup fresh lemon juice

⅓ cup Worcestershire sauce

2 teaspoons prepared horseradish

2 teaspoons Tabasco or other hot sauce (optional)

2 teaspoons celery salt

1 teaspoon ground black pepper

Combine the lemon juice, Worcestershire sauce, horseradish, and hot sauce, if desired, in a jar. Add the celery salt and pepper and mix well. To serve, combine tomato juice and vodka, if desired, in a glass over ice. Stir in 1 to 3 tablespoons of the concentrate, depending upon how spicy you like your Bloody Mary. Add a stalk of celery or pickled green bean.

Makes about ¾ cup.

Note: This mix will keep for months in a sealed jar in the refrigerator.

Ceviche—More or less like it is made in northern Mexico.

1 pound fresh fish fillets (nonoily, such as red snapper, pompano, or sole), finely diced
1 cup ReaLemon juice
1 large yellow onion, finely chopped
1 jalapeño pepper, cored, seeded, deveined, and finely chopped
1 teaspoon dried oregano
Salt and ground black pepper to taste
¼ cup olive oil
2 medium tomatoes, chopped

Place the fish in a glass or ceramic bowl, add the lemon juice, taking care to immerse all the fish in the juice, cover, and let sit for 1 hour at room temperature. Drain and rinse the fish with cold water. Combine in a serving bowl with the onion, jalapeño pepper, oregano, salt, and pepper. Cover and chill in the refrigerator. Before serving, mix in the oil and tomatoes. Serve as a salad or as hors d'oeuvres on whole-wheat crackers or Belgian endive leaves.

Serves 10 as hors d'oeuvres or 6 as a salad.

Note: Fresh fish is the key to great ceviche. One of our authors actually takes the mixings and crackers out in the boat, and makes the ceviche after the first fish is caught! One hour later he is eating it. What a great snack for a fishing trip!

Con Queso Dip—A historical winner.

1 pound Velveeta cheese
½ cup hot *picante* sauce
¼ teaspoon Tabasco or other hot sauce
2 whole jalapeño peppers, slit open and seeded

Put the cheese in a 1-quart microwave-safe dish and microwave at full power to melt, about 5 minutes, stirring midway through. Stir in the *picante* sauce and hot sauce. Garnish with the jalapeño peppers.

Makes 2½ cups.

Note: Serve with fresh vegetables or whole-grain chips for dipping.

Crab Dip—Your guests will like this one.

One 8-ounce package Philadelphia Light or
  other light cream cheese
One 10¾-ounce can cream of mushroom soup
½ cup no sugar added yogurt
2 tablespoons mayonnaise
8 small green onions, trimmed and chopped
2 large stalks celery, finely chopped
One 6½-ounce can crabmeat or 6 ounces
  cooked fresh lump crabmeat, cartilage and
  shell picked out
Hot sauce to taste (optional)

In a bowl, mix together the cream cheese and
soup until smooth. Mix in the yogurt, mayonnaise, green onions, celery, crabmeat, and hot
sauce, if desired. Cover and chill for 2 hours in
the refrigerator or 20 minutes in the freezer.

Serves 10 to 12.

Note: Serve with whole-grain crackers.

Curry Vegetable Dip—Very versatile for any number of vegetables.

1 cup reduced-fat sour cream
½ cup mayonnaise
1 tablespoon fresh lemon juice
2 tablespoons chopped fresh parsley
2 tablespoon grated white onion
1 tablespoon minced chives
2 tablespoons prepared yellow mustard
1 teaspoon curry powder
½ teaspoon paprika
½ teaspoon dried tarragon
Salt and ground black pepper to taste
Several dashes of Tabasco or other hot sauce

In a bowl, blend the sour cream, mayonnaise, and lemon juice. Mix in the parsley, onion, chives, mustard, curry powder, paprika, tarragon, salt, and pepper. Add hot sauce to taste, cover, and chill for at least 1 hour in the refrigerator or 15 minutes in the freezer.

Makes about 1¾ cups.

Note: Serve with fresh vegetables as a dip.

Deviled Eggs—Nutritious enough to be almost a meal in itself.

6 hard-boiled eggs
2 tablespoons mayonnaise
1 teaspoon vinegar
½ teaspoon dry mustard
¼ teaspoon salt
¼ teaspoon paprika
⅛ teaspoon ground black pepper

Cut the eggs in half lengthwise. Remove the yolks, reserving the egg whites. Put the yolks into a bowl. Mash and mix in the mayonnaise, vinegar, dry mustard, salt, paprika, and pepper. Divide the mixture among the cavities of the whites. Cover and refrigerate until well chilled.

Makes 12 deviled eggs.

Note: Good served with a salad or as an hors d'oeuvre. They hold up well if you want to make them in advance of a party; tightly wrapped, the eggs can be stored in the refrigerator for up to 24 hours.

Oyster Ramakis—A seafood version of ramakis, usually made with livers.

12 slices bacon, halved
24 fresh oysters, shucked
2 tablespoons chopped fresh parsley
½ teaspoon salt
Cayenne pepper to taste
Ground black pepper to taste

Preheat the broiler. Lay one oyster on each strip of bacon. Top each with ¼ teaspoon parsley, and sprinkle with salt, cayenne pepper, and black pepper. Roll the bacon strips up around the oysters. Place the ramakis on a broiler tray, position about 4 inches from the heat source, and broil until well browned, 7 to 8 minutes. Turn carefully and broil until the bacon is very crisp, 3 to 4 minutes.

Makes 24 individual appetizers.

Note: The ramakis could also serve 4 as a light entrée. As hors d'oeuvres, stick a toothpick into each to make them easier to eat.

Oysters Tony—Another homegrown recipe.
Has a contagious taste.

1 stick butter

8 green onions, trimmed and cut into ½-inch
   pieces

½ pound white button mushrooms, ends
   trimmed and halved

½ teaspoon garlic salt plus additional to taste

3 dozen fresh oysters, shucked

½ cup dry vermouth

Tabasco or other hot sauce to taste

Melt the butter in a large skillet over medium
heat. Add the green onions and mushrooms.
Sprinkle with garlic salt and cook, stirring, until the vegetables begin to become soft, about
3 minutes. Add the oysters and continue to
cook until they begin to curl around the edge,
about 3 minutes. Add the vermouth and boil for
1 to 2 minutes, until a sauce forms. Spoon oysters, onions, and mushrooms onto Triscuit or
Finn Crisp crackers. Garnish each cracker with a
drop or more of hot sauce and sprinkle with
more garlic salt if desired.

Serves 10.

Note: This dish can also be a main course meal for 4. Serve in a bowl and eat with a fork and spoon. Serve without crackers, but don't forget the hot sauce! The juice left over in the saucepan is a high-quality oyster soup.

Mock Oysters—For the nonoyster lovers.

1 stick butter
8 medium green onions, trimmed and chopped
½ pound white button mushrooms, chopped
¼ cup garlic cheese (such as Boursin)
One 10¾-ounce can cream of mushroom soup
One 10-ounce package frozen chopped broccoli,
    thawed
½ teaspoon salt
¼ teaspoon ground black pepper

Melt the butter in a medium skillet over medium-high heat. Add the green onions and mushrooms, and sauté until the onion turns translucent, 2 to 3 minutes. Add the cheese, soup, broccoli, salt, and pepper. Mix well and continue to cook for 1 to 2 minutes to heat through.

Serves 10.

Note: Serve with whole-wheat crackers or whole-grain chips. You could also add a second package of broccoli and serve as a vegetable side dish for 6 to 8.

Appetizers and Hors d'oeuvres

Spicy Oysters—A sure hit hors d'oeuvre.

¼ cup butter

1 quart shucked fresh oysters in their juice

2 slices bacon, crisp cooked and crumbled

2 cloves garlic, crushed

1 tablespoon Lea & Perrins or other
    Worcestershire sauce

1 teaspoon Tabasco or other hot sauce

½ teaspoon celery salt

½ teaspoon Tony Cachere's Creole Seasoning

Combine the butter, oysters, bacon, and garlic in a large skillet over medium heat. Add the Worcestershire sauce, hot sauce, celery salt, and Creole seasoning and simmer until almost all the liquid has been absorbed, 3 to 4 minutes.

Serves 10 to 12.

Note: Serve in a heated chafing dish with toothpicks.

Cherry Tomatoes and Prosciutto—Tomatoes and ham; always a winner.

¼ cup grated Parmesan cheese

1 tablespoon chopped fresh flat-leaf parsley

Salt to taste

¼ lemon

1 dozen ripe cherry tomatoes, trimmed and halved

4 to 5 slices prosciutto ham, thinly sliced

In a bowl, mix together the Parmesan cheese, parsley, and salt. Squeeze 2 or 3 drops of lemon juice onto each tomato half, and top with ¼ teaspoon of the Parmesan mixture. Fold 1-by-3-inch strips of prosciutto in half lengthwise, and wrap each up around a tomato half, securing with toothpicks.

Makes 24 individual appetizers.

Note: For a taste variation, replace the parsley with chopped fresh basil.

Tuna and Cheese Spread

One 3-ounce package reduced-fat cream cheese
⅓ cup sour cream
One 7-ounce can white tuna packed in water,
  drained
3 tablespoons minced green onion
3 tablespoons chopped celery
2 tablespoons chopped ripe olives
½ cup chopped pecans
Salt and ground black pepper to taste

In a bowl, mix the cream cheese and sour cream
with a fork until smooth. Mix in the tuna, green
onion, celery, and olives. Fold in the pecans.
Add salt and pepper to taste. Press the mixture
into a ball or mold it into a shape of your choice.
Cover and chill in the refrigerator for 2 hours or
in the freezer for 12 to 15 minutes.

Serves 12.

Note: Serve on a large lettuce leaf or leaves,
with any type of whole-wheat crackers on the
side. This one will give your guests a nice portion of omega-3 fatty acids.

IX | Salad Dressings, Sauces, and Stocks

Almost any type of lettuce can satisfy your palate if delicately coated with the proper salad dressing. We offer you a variety of dressings to help you achieve gastronomical enjoyment from your salads while receiving the side benefits of the fiber and roughage contained in these very low-glycemic carbohydrates.

Eating a lot of salads, often accompanied by raw cauliflower, broccoli, tomatoes, cucumbers, squash, onions, and the like, will provide you not only with fiber but also the additional benefit of a lot of the antioxidant vitamins A, C, and E in their natural forms.

The taste of an otherwise plain piece of meat or a steamed vegetable can be tremendously enhanced by the addition of a warm, savory sauce that is added to, or sometimes cooked with, the dish in question. While some sauces are inherently rich in saturated fat, many can be modified to remove some of this type of fat while still allowing retention of the good flavor.

We cannot overstress the flavor enhancing potential of beef, chicken, or fish stocks. If you will keep one or more of them on hand, you will find that you will use them successfully, in place of water, for simply steaming broccoli, cauliflower, squash, and the like. Homemade stocks can even be used as the liquid in which you boil your various greens or peas.

Salad Dressings, Sauces, and Stocks Recipes

Salad Dressings

Caesar Dressing, page 307

Blue Cheese Dressing, page 308

Quick French Dressing, page 309

Mustard-Based Dressing, page 310

Ranch Dressing, page 311

Roquefort Dressing, page 312

Balsamic Vinaigrette, page 313

Cider Vinaigrette, page 314

Sauces

Béarnaise Sauce, page 315

Hollandaise Sauce, page 317

Hollandaise Sauce in Blender, page 318

Hot Fish Sauce, page 319

Marinara Sauce, page 320

Meunière Sauce, page 321

Basic Pasta Sauce, page 322

Remoulade Sauce, page 323

Salsa, page 324

Basic Tomato Sauce, page 325

Basic Broths (Stocks), page 327

Caesar Dressing

½ cup mayonnaise

2 tablespoons fresh lemon juice

1 teaspoon anchovy paste

1 teaspoon Dijon mustard

½ teaspoon ground black pepper

2 cloves garlic, peeled

Combine the mayonnaise, lemon juice, anchovy paste, mustard, and pepper in a small bowl. Press in the garlic and whisk until smooth.

Makes about ⅔ cup.

Note: If you happen to have some anchovies on hand, by all means use them for an even more flavorful dressing. Substitute 4 anchovy fillets, minced, for the anchovy paste.

Blue Cheese Dressing—The fresh blue cheese is the secret of this one.

½ cup extra virgin olive oil

3 tablespoons white wine vinegar

½ teaspoon garlic powder

½ teaspoon onion powder

½ teaspoon dried tarragon

½ teaspoon dried chervil

½ teaspoon Italian seasoning

½ teaspoon coarse ground black pepper

½ cup crumbled fresh blue cheese

Combine the oil, vinegar, garlic powder, onion powder, tarragon, chervil, Italian seasoning, and pepper in a jar. Seal and shake vigorously to blend. Just before serving, add the blue cheese, reseal, and shake the jar once or twice. Pour over the salad and serve immediately.

Makes about 1¼ cups.

Note: This dressing is the key to our Mixed Green Salad with Grapes (page 356).

Quick French Dressing—Quick! Instant! As close as you will get.

⅔ cup canola oil
⅓ cup apple cider vinegar
1 teaspoon salt
½ teaspoon paprika
¼ teaspoon ground black pepper
½ packet artificial sweetener

Combine the oil, vinegar, salt, paprika, pepper, and artificial sweetener in a jar. Shake well (before each use).

Makes about 1 cup.

Note: This dressing is very good on Easy Avocado (page 220). For a creamier French dressing, blend for 1 minute in a blender or mini–food processor.

Mustard-Based Dressing—Oil and vinegar with some seasoning!

1 heaping tablespoon Creole or Dijon mustard
¼ cup red wine vinegar
1 cup extra virgin olive oil
¼ cup minced green bell pepper (optional)

Put the mustard into a small bowl. Whisk in the vinegar, then the oil. Stir in the bell pepper, if desired.

Makes about 1¼ cups.

Note: Try this on Instant Asparagus (page 219) in place of French dressing.

Ranch Dressing

1 cup buttermilk
2 teaspoons olive oil
2 tablespoons fresh lemon juice
4 drops hot sauce
2 tablespoons chopped fresh cilantro
1 teaspoon chili powder
⅛ teaspoon ground white pepper
Dash of salt

In a small bowl, whisk together the buttermilk, oil, lemon juice, hot sauce, cilantro, chili powder, white pepper, and salt.

Makes about 1 cup.

Note: This spicy dressing goes well with any green salad.

Roquefort Dressing—A very popular dressing.

2 tablespoons Roquefort cheese

1 cup mayonnaise

Juice of ½ lemon

1 tablespoon Worcestershire sauce

1 teaspoon prepared horseradish

1 teaspoon garlic salt

Dash of cayenne pepper

Put the cheese into a small bowl. Cream with a fork. Add the mayonnaise, then the lemon juice, Worcestershire sauce, horseradish, garlic salt, and cayenne pepper.

Makes about 1 generous cup.

Note: Good at room temperature or when chilled.

Balsamic Vinaigrette—Always a winner!

½ cup olive oil

3½ teaspoons balsamic vinegar

1 tablespoon water

2 teaspoons minced green onion (dark green
   tops trimmed off)

½ to 1 packet artificial sweetener (to taste)

Pinch of ground cumin (or more to taste)

Salt and ground black pepper to taste

Combine the oil, vinegar, water, green onion, artificial sweetener, cumin, salt, and pepper in a jar. Shake well (before each use). Serve chilled.

Makes about ⅔ cup.

Note: When used with a spinach salad, add toasted sliced walnuts and crumbled blue cheese as a garnish.

Cider Vinaigrette—Goes well with spinach salad!

¼ cup olive oil
Juice of ½ lemon
1 tablespoon apple cider vinegar
1 clove garlic, mashed
¼ teaspoon Lawry's or other seasoned salt
⅛ teaspoon ground black pepper

In a small bowl, whisk together the oil, lemon juice, vinegar, garlic, seasoned salt, and pepper.

Makes about 1 cup.

Note: This is good on almost any type of green salad.

Salad Dressings, Sauces, and Stocks

Béarnaise Sauce—Another historic hit.

1 pound (4 sticks) butter
½ cup dry white wine
1 teaspoon dried tarragon
4 egg yolks
2 teaspoons fresh lemon juice
¾ teaspoon Tabasco or other hot sauce
¾ teaspoon Worcestershire sauce

Melt the butter in a 1-quart saucepan over low heat. Raise the heat to medium and bring to a boil. Remove from the heat and skim, then return to the lowest possible heat to keep warm. Combine the wine and tarragon in a small skillet. Cook over high heat until the volume of liquid in the pan has been reduced to about 2 tablespoons. Put about 1 inch of water into the bottom of a double boiler. In the top, whisk together in the wine reduction, egg yolks, lemon juice, hot sauce, and Worcestershire sauce. Bring the water in the bottom to a simmer, taking care not to let it bubble up enough to touch the bottom of the upper pan. Whisking constantly, simmer until the sauce begins to thicken, about 5 minutes. Still whisking, drizzle in the butter, and continue to whisk until the mixture is thick and creamy.

Makes about 2 cups.

Note: This sauce does contain butter! Fortunately, a modest topping of béarnaise sauce goes a long way in adding flavor to Poached Salmon (page 196) and is also good on Texas Steak (page 203).

Hollandaise Sauce—Please learn to prepare and use this one.

½ pound (2 sticks) butter
4 egg yolks
2 tablespoons fresh lemon juice
¼ teaspoon salt
⅛ teaspoon ground white pepper

Put about 1 inch of water into the bottom of a double boiler and bring to a simmer. Meanwhile, put the butter in a 1-quart saucepan and heat just at the bubbling stage for 1 minute over medium heat. Remove from the heat and skim, then return to the lowest possible heat to keep warm. Over medium-low heat, whisk together the eggs, lemon juice, salt, and pepper in the top of the double boiler until the sauce begins to thicken, about 3 minutes, taking care not to let the water bubble up enough to touch the bottom of the upper pan. Whisking constantly, drizzle in the butter, continuing to whisk to a smooth, creamy consistency.

Makes about 1 cup.

Note: Serve hollandaise warm from the pan, when it is always best. Hollandaise is particularly good over eggs (see page 65 and 67), asparagus, or broccoli.

Hollandaise Sauce in Blender—A shortcut to making hollandaise.

1 stick butter
4 egg yolks
2 tablespoons fresh lemon juice
½ teaspoon salt
Pinch of cayenne pepper

Heat the butter just until bubbly in a small pan over medium-low heat. Meanwhile, combine the egg yolks, lemon juice, salt, and cayenne pepper in a blender. Turn the machine on and add the butter in a slow, steady stream until incorporated and thickened.

Makes about 1 cup.

Note: If you have time, the longer version is somewhat more pleasing to the palate.

Hot Fish Sauce—A homemade recipe that works!

½ pound (2 sticks) butter or margarine
2 tablespoons chopped fresh parsley
2 tablespoons chili sauce
1 tablespoon plus 1 teaspoon fresh lemon juice
2 teaspoons Worcestershire sauce
2 teaspoons Dijon mustard
2 drops Tabasco or other hot sauce

Melt the butter in a 1-quart saucepan over medium heat. Add the parsley, chili sauce, lemon juice, Worcestershire sauce, mustard, and hot sauce. Stir and heat until bubbly, about 4 minutes.

Makes about 1¼ cups.

Note: This sauce works well on any grilled nonoily fish. Make sure both the fish and the sauce are hot when served.

Marinara Sauce—Good with many pastas.

¼ cup olive oil
1 large yellow onion, chopped
4 cloves garlic, minced
6 medium tomatoes, seeded and diced
2 tablespoons chopped fresh basil
1 teaspoon dried oregano
½ teaspoon salt
Dash of cayenne pepper

Combine the oil, onion, and garlic in a large nonstick skillet over medium heat. Stirring constantly, cook until the onion turns translucent, about 5 minutes. Add the tomatoes, basil, oregano, salt, and cayenne pepper. Cook at a low boil until the tomatoes have begun to break down to form a thick, chunky sauce, about 20 minutes. Serve warm.

Makes about 5 cups.

Note: For seafood pasta, fold chopped, cooked shrimp into the sauce after it has thickened, and cook for a minute or two more to warm through.

Meunière Sauce—Great for delicate fish.

1 cup fish stock
1 clove garlic, minced
¾ pound (3 sticks) butter
2 tablespoons stone-ground whole-wheat flour
¼ cup Worcestershire sauce
¼ teaspoon salt

Combine the stock and garlic in a medium saucepan. Bring to a boil over medium-high heat, remove from the heat, and set aside. Melt ½ stick of the butter in a small skillet over medium heat. Stir in the flour and cook for about 30 seconds, until blended. Stir the butter and flour mixture into the stock. Return the saucepan to the stove top over medium heat. Stir in the remaining 2½ sticks butter, then the Worcestershire sauce and salt. Stirring constantly, cook until the sauce begins to thicken, about 5 minutes. Serve hot over hot fish.

Makes about 2 cups.

Note: Lemon wedges or sliced lemon rounds make a nice garnish for fish topped with this sauce.

Basic Pasta Sauce—Nothing fancy here!

2 tablespoons olive oil
1 medium white onion, chopped
¼ cup chopped fresh flat-leaf parsley
One 28-ounce can crushed tomatoes in purée
4 cloves garlic, minced
1 stalk celery, minced
1 teaspoon dried basil
½ teaspoon dried oregano
1 teaspoon salt
¾ teaspoon ground black pepper

Combine the oil, onion, and parsley in a large saucepan over medium-high heat. Sauté until the onion turns translucent, 2 to 3 minutes. Stir in the tomatoes, garlic, celery, basil, oregano, salt, and pepper. Bring to a boil, then reduce the heat to medium-low and simmer until thickened, about 20 minutes.

Makes about 3½ cups.

Note: If you wish to add meat to the sauce, cut it into bite-size pieces and brown well. Add the meat to the sauce after sautéeing the onion and parsley and increase the amount of time the sauce simmers to about 30 minutes. Served over pasta made from stone-ground whole-wheat flour, this would serve 4 to 6.

*Remoulade Sauce—A must if you like shrimp
and crabmeat.*

⅔ cup olive oil
½ cup Creole mustard
¼ cup apple cider vinegar
2 green onions (bulbs only), finely sliced
2 cloves garlic, minced
1 tablespoon paprika
1 teaspoon salt
½ teaspoon cayenne pepper

In a food processor or blender, combine the
oil, mustard, vinegar, green onions, garlic, paprika, salt, and cayenne pepper. Purée, transfer
to a bowl, cover, and chill before serving.

Makes about 1⅔ cups.

Note: This sauce also goes well with cold meats.

Salsa—Very simple but ranks with the best of them.

One 10-ounce can RO•TEL diced tomatoes
    and chilies
½ cup chopped medium white onion
¼ cup finely chopped fresh cilantro
Juice of ½ lemon
Salt to taste

Combine the tomatoes, onion, cilantro, and lemon juice in a bowl. Add salt, if desired, and mix well.

Makes about 1½ cups.

Note: This salsa can be served with beans, meats, eggs, or even guacamole salad.

Basic Tomato Sauce—A good sauce for many different pastas.

3 tablespoons extra virgin olive oil
1 medium white onion, chopped
3 cloves garlic, finely chopped
One 28-ounce can crushed tomatoes in purée
One 15-ounce can no sugar added tomato sauce
   in purée
½ cup chopped fresh basil or 1 teaspoon dried
   basil
1 teaspoon baking soda
½ teaspoon salt
Ground black pepper to taste

Combine the oil, onion, and garlic in a medium skillet over medium heat. Stirring constantly, cook until the onion turns translucent, 3 to 4 minutes. Stir in the tomatoes and tomato sauce, then the basil and baking soda. When the sauce begins to bubble gently, reduce the heat to medium-low. Stirring frequently, simmer until thickened, about 15 minutes. Season with salt and pepper.

Makes about 5 cups.

Note: This is a universal sauce for meat, fish, or pasta. If you like added spice, substitute ⅛ teaspoon crushed red pepper flakes for the black pepper.

Basic Broths (Stocks)—Easy and always better than canned.

3 quarts water

3 yellow onions, quartered

3 cloves garlic, mashed (optional)

3 stalks celery, chopped

About 6 pounds chicken neck, back, leg, or wing bones with meat scraps, browned; or about 6 pounds beef with lean meat scraps, browned; or 3 to 4 pounds fish carcasses (without heads) and/or shrimp or crab shells

Combine the water, onions, garlic, celery, and chicken bones, or beef bones, or fish carcasses and/or shells in a large stockpot. Bring to a boil, then lower the heat to maintain a bare simmer. Cook up to 4 hours (but only about 1 hour for fast-cooking fish stock). Strain and refrigerate. For chicken or beef broth, skim congealed fat from the surface before using.

Makes 6 to 8 cups.

Note: You can often get the needed bones or carcasses from your butcher or fish market.

X | Snacks

Most snacks really do not require recipes. We have included this section, however, because snacks play an important role in the SUGAR BUSTERS! lifestyle. Consumption of a good snack will often prevent you from becoming so ravenous when you do not eat as regularly as you would like. Delayed meals are usually the ones where you tend to go back to the trough and consume more than you should.

Snacks play another important role. Snack time gives you the opportunity to consume a nutritious piece of fruit that you may have skipped earlier in the day because of your busy schedule, or that you may not want to consume with your planned red meat dinner. This is also a good time to drink several glasses of water or a glass of fresh juice that will also keep you from overeating.

Snacks give you the opportunity to consume that piece of chocolate you still desire, and do it at a time when there is nothing else to interfere with your total glycemic response, and when you can fully enjoy it all by itself! Remember not to eat too much chocolate and to find yourself a high cocoa content chocolate (60 percent or more cocoa) that does not contain so much added sugar. Finally, be extra careful of low-fat snack bars. Most are full of added sugar.

Snack Suggestions

Cheese or Meat Dip on some type of whole-grain cracker

Fresh Fruit—comes ready to eat; no recipe required!

Fresh Vegetables—Broccoli, Cauliflower, Celery, Cucumber, Cherry Tomatoes, Zucchini, etc.

Fresh Vegetables and Cheese Dip—above vegetables with your favorite cheese dip

100 percent Fruit Jam on 3 or 4 whole-grain crackers

Raw Nuts

Roasted Nuts—Simply toast and eat, or add salt and/or red or black pepper

No Sugar Added Peanut Butter—eaten by itself or spread on a whole-wheat cracker, celery stick, etc.

Chocolate—2 or 3 bites of high cocoa content (60 percent or more) chocolate

Coffee—flavored, no sugar added, regular or decaf coffee

Hard-Boiled Eggs

Cheese Bites

Leftover Steak, Pork, Lamb, Chicken, or Turkey Bites

Yogurt—no sugar added

XI | Desserts

For many people, the most difficult part of adhering to the SUGAR BUSTERS! lifestyle comes at dessert time. Fortunately, after a few weeks of eliminating or severely restricting your consumption of refined sugar, the craving for sweet desserts drops dramatically. This is true for most people, but certainly not all.

The general way of eating as presented in the SUGAR BUSTERS! lifestyle came from studying the many benefits of eating less refined sugar and fewer highly processed grain products as they do in France and the Mediterranean area. Why not take their lead and follow a meal with dessert of a simple green salad coated with a subtle olive oil and mild herb dressing or a few bites of cheese?

Another good way to end a meal if you feel the sweet craving coming on, is to eat a few nuts such as almonds, walnuts, or pecans. Nuts contain fat which our taste buds also like. Fortunately, the primary fat in most nuts is not saturated fat, but monounsaturated fat, which is the type that tends to increase the ratio of HDL (good) cholesterol versus the LDL (bad) cholesterol. This relatively small consumption of nuts does satisfy most people's desire for a little something extra following a nice meal.

Desserts

Dessert Recipes

BAPS (Browned Apple Patties), page 334
Goochi Apples, page 335
Egg Custard, page 336
Dessert Pecans, page 337
Sweet Potato Pecan Balls, page 338
Vanilla Ice Cream, page 340
Low-Sugar Lemon Crêpes, page 342

BAPS (Browned Apple Patties)—A nutritious, low-glycemic dessert.

2 medium-size firm cooking apples, peeled,
  cored, and grated
½ cup chopped pecans, walnuts, or almonds
3 tablespoons stone-ground whole-wheat flour
4 packets fructose sweetener
¼ teaspoon fresh lemon juice
2 tablespoons butter

Combine the apples, nuts, flour, fructose sweetener, and lemon juice in a bowl. Mix and form into 4 patties. Melt the butter in a medium nonstick skillet over medium-low heat. Add the patties, and cook until firm and lightly browned, about 5 minutes. Turn them over carefully, and cook until browned on the other side, about 5 minutes more.

Serves 4.

Note: Eat this dessert following a meal of fish, chicken, or low-glycemic carbohydrates. If you have really had a modest size, low-fat meal, serve the warm patties with 1 scoop of no sugar added vanilla ice cream.

Goochi Apples—A New Orleans creation.

2 medium Golden Delicious apples (unpeeled),
  cored and cut into chunks
One 8-ounce can unsweetened pineapple
  chunks (in own juice)
½ cup seedless grapes
1 satsuma orange, peeled and sectioned
  (optional)
½ cup orange juice
¼ teaspoon ground cinnamon
1 tablespoon butter, cut into pieces

Preheat the oven to 350 degrees. In a 7-by-11-inch baking dish, combine the apples, pineapple with its own juice, grapes, and satsuma, if desired. Drizzle with the orange juice and sprinkle with the cinnamon. Add the butter, stir, and cover. Bake just until the apples are tender, 20 to 30 minutes.

Serves 4.

Note: This is not a particularly low-glycemic dessert, but it is a good one and may be eaten occasionally.

Egg Custard—Flavor it any way you like.

3 large eggs
4 packets artificial sweetener (Do not use
   Equal.)
¼ teaspoon salt
2 cups milk
¼ teaspoon vanilla extract
⅛ teaspoon grated nutmeg

Preheat the oven to 350 degrees. Beat the eggs in a large bowl. Stir in the artificial sweetener and salt, then the milk, vanilla, and nutmeg. Divide the mixture among six 4-ounce custard cups. Set the cups in a large baking dish and add enough hot water to fill the dish with 1 inch of water. Bake until set, about 30 minutes. Serve warm, room temperature, or chilled.

Serves 6.

Note: If you prefer, use cinnamon instead of nutmeg. For Vanilla Custard, boost the amount of vanilla extract to 1 teaspoon.

Dessert Pecans—For handy snacks following a meal.

2 cups water
1 cup pecan halves
10 packets artificial sweetener (Do not use
    Equal)
1 cup canola oil
Salt to taste

Bring the water to a boil in a 1-quart saucepan. Add the pecans, boil for 1 minute, then drain well. Transfer the pecans to a bowl, and toss with the artificial sweetener to coat thoroughly. Heat the oil in a large skillet over medium heat. Add the pecans and sauté, stirring constantly or shaking the pan, until the nuts have turned dark brown, 4 to 5 minutes. Using a slotted spoon, remove the nuts to wax paper or paper towels to drain. Sprinkle with salt, and eat slightly warm or at room temperature.

Serves 8.

Note: Raw pecans are also good for dessert. The fat, dominantly monounsaturated, seems to satisfy most people's sweet tooth within 5 minutes of consumption. When sautéing the pecans, take care not to let them burn.

Sweet Potato Pecan Balls—An extremely nutritious dessert.

1 medium sweet potato, scrubbed
2 tablespoons whipped butter
8 pecan halves, chopped
1 or 2 packets artificial sweetener or fructose
1 teaspoon ground cinnamon
Salt to taste

Preheat the broiler. Wrap the potato in a paper towel and microwave at full power for 4 to 5 minutes, until soft to the touch. Slice open, remove the pulp with a spoon, and put it into a bowl. While still hot, mix in the butter. Add the pecans, artificial sweetener or fructose, and cinnamon. Mix thoroughly and form the mixture into 8 balls about 1½ inches in diameter. Place on a baking sheet that has been sprayed with nonstick cooking spray. Position about 4 inches from the heat source, and broil until somewhat crusty, 2 to 3 minutes. Turn the balls over, and broil for about 2 minutes more to brown the other side. Sprinkle with salt and serve.

Serves 2 to 4.

Desserts

Note: Also try these as a side dish with roast turkey. Sweet potatoes are extremely nutritious, containing well over the recommended daily allowance of beta-carotene. Whipped butter contains about 30 percent less saturated fat than an equivalent amount of regular butter.

Vanilla Ice Cream—The richer the mix, the lower the glycemic index.

6 egg yolks
1 quart (4 cups) whole milk
1 cup Equal Spoonful sweetener
½ teaspoon salt
1 quart heavy cream
2 tablespoons vanilla extract

Beat the egg yolks and pour them into a 3-quart saucepan. Stir in the milk, Equal Spoonful, and salt. Stirring constantly with a wooden spoon, cook over low heat until the mixture lightly coats the back of the spoon, about 15 minutes. Remove the pan from the heat and allow to cool for 10 minutes. Stir in the cream and vanilla. Chill the mixture in the freezer for about 15 minutes. Pour into an electric or manual ice-cream maker and process according to manufacturer's directions.

Makes about 2 quarts, or enough to serve 10 to 12.

Note: This is not a low-fat dessert! However, neither is it a high-glycemic index dessert. If you know you will be making ice cream on a given day, plan your other meals to be very low in saturated fat. And as with many vanilla ice-cream recipes, peaches, strawberries, or other fruits can be added while cooking and freezing. Eating ice cream *every day* is not a good idea if you are trying to lose weight! Make yourself some meringue cookies with the leftover egg whites.

Low-Sugar Lemon Crêpes—A great occasional dessert; worth the effort.

Filling:

Three 8-ounce packages cream cheese, at room
   temperature
5½ teaspoons (22 packets) artificial sweetener
1½ tablespoons rum
Juice of 1½ lemons
1½ tablespoons grated lemon zest (peel)

To make the filling, put the cream cheese into a mixing bowl or a food processor. Beat with an electric mixer or process until smooth and fluffy. While continuing to beat, gradually add the artificial sweetener. Beat in the rum, lemon juice, and lemon zest. (You should have about 3 cups of the filling.) Set aside.

Batter:

6 large eggs, beaten
2½ tablespoons butter, melted
1 cup whole milk
¼ teaspoon vanilla extract
½ teaspoon salt
1¼ cups stone-ground whole-wheat flour

For the batter, combine the eggs, butter, milk, vanilla, and salt in a blender. Add the flour and blend until smooth. The batter should be thick enough to lightly coat a spoon. If it is too thick, add a little water; if too thin, a little flour. (The batter will thicken on its own as it sits.) Preheat a small nonstick skillet over medium heat. Lightly grease with canola oil before adding batter. Using about 2 tablespoons for each, cook 20 to 24 crêpes, pouring the batter to thinly cover the bottom of the skillet, and cooking until the crêpe turns lightly brown on the bottom and small holes dot the surface, about 1 minute. Turn the crêpe over and cook for 30 seconds on the other side. Transfer the crêpes to a platter as cooked and cover with plastic wrap to keep tender.

Lemon Butter Sauce:

¾ pound (3 sticks) butter
9 packets artificial sweetener
¾ cup fresh lemon juice
1½ tablespoons grated lemon zest (peel)

For the sauce, melt the butter in a 1-quart saucepan over low heat. Stir in the artificial sweetener until dissolved. Stir in the lemon juice and lemon zest, and cook for about 1 minute more to heat through.

Assembly:

¼ cup plus 2 tablespoons brandy (3 ounces)

To assemble, fill the center of each crêpe with 2 tablespoons of the filling and fold up like an envelope. Warm the sauce in a large skillet or chafing dish. Add the assembled crêpes side by side, seam side up. Cook for 1 to 2 minutes over medium-low heat, then turn the crêpes seam-side down. Drizzle the brandy and swirl the pan to coat the crêpes evenly. Carefully ignite and allow the alcohol to burn off. Serve 2 crêpes per person on warmed dessert dishes, spooning warm sauce over the crêpes.

Serves 10 to 12 (20 to 24 crêpes).

Note: You can make the batter, filling, and sauce ahead of time but remember to warm everything prior to serving.

XII | Holiday Menus

Thanksgiving Dinner for 12, page 346

Christmas Dinner for 8, page 354

Hanukkah Dinner for 8, page 358

New Year's Day Dinner for 6, page 361

Easter Supper for 8, page 364

Passover Seder for 8, page 366

Summer Holiday Barbecue for 6 to 8, page 369

Thanksgiving Dinner for 12

Turkey with Natural Gravy
(recipe follows)

Veal and Pork Dressing with Chopped Pecans
(recipe follows)

No Sugar Added Cranberry Relish
(recipe follows)

Sweet Potato Lyonnaise
(triple recipe)
from *SUGAR BUSTERS! Cut Sugar to Trim Fat*
page 221

Fresh Green Bean and Pimiento Bundles
(recipe follows)

Green Peas with Tiny Pearl Onions
(recipe follows)

Fresh Spinach Salad with Bacon
(triple recipe)
(see page 119)

Goochi Apples
(triple recipe)
(see page 335)

Turkey with Natural Gravy

One 12-pound fresh turkey or frozen turkey,
   thawed
1¾ teaspoons salt
¾ teaspoon ground black pepper
¼ cup plus 2 tablespoons whipped butter, at
   room temperature
¾ teaspoon paprika
½ teaspoon dried thyme
⅛ teaspoon cayenne pepper
2½ cups chicken broth
3 tablespoons stone-ground whole-wheat flour

Preheat the oven to 325 degrees. Remove the
giblets, rinse the turkey well inside and out, and
pat dry. Trim off all visible fat. Rub the body
and neck cavities with ¾ teaspoon of the salt
and the black pepper. Place on a rack in a roasting
pan. In a small bowl, combine the butter, paprika, thyme, cayenne pepper, and the remaining 1 teaspoon salt. Rub the bird all over to coat
with the mixture. Cover with aluminum foil.
Roast for 2 hours and 15 minutes, remove the
aluminum foil, and roast until the bird is crisp
and golden brown and the meatiest part of the
thigh has reached an internal temperature of

180 degrees, about 45 minutes more. Remove the turkey to a cutting board and let sit for 15 minutes before carving. Meanwhile, to make the gravy, pour the pan juices into a large measuring cup. Add enough broth to make 3 cups. Place the roasting pan on the stove top over medium-low heat and sprinkle the flour over the bottom of the pan. Stirring constantly, cook for 1 minute. While stirring, pour in the broth mixture and cook until thickened, about 3 minutes.

Veal and Pork Dressing with Chopped Pecans

(Can be prepared ahead of time.)

2 pounds ground veal

1 pound ground pork

1 turkey liver or 2 chicken livers, chopped
 (optional)

1 stick butter

2 large yellow onions, chopped

4 stalks celery, chopped

8 green onions, trimmed and chopped

3 tablespoons chopped fresh parsley

½ teaspoon dried thyme

3 bay leaves

4 cups whole-grain whole-wheat bread crumbs

2 cups coarsely chopped pecans

3 large eggs, beaten

1 teaspoon salt

½ teaspoon ground black pepper

Preheat the oven to 325 degrees. Combine the veal, pork, and liver, if desired, in a large skillet and cook over medium heat, stirring constantly until browned, about 10 minutes. Using a slotted spoon, remove the meat to a large bowl. Drain the fat and add the butter to the skillet.

When it has melted, add the onions, celery, and green onions. Stirring, cook until the onions turn translucent, 3 to 4 minutes. Stir in the parsley, thyme, and bay leaves. Continue to cook, stirring frequently, until the vegetables are soft, about 5 minutes. Scrape the mixture into the bowl with the meat. Stir well. In a second bowl, add just enough water to the bread crumbs to moisten, then squeeze out excess water and add moistened bread crumbs to the meat mixture. Stir well. Stir in the pecans, then the eggs. Season with salt and pepper. Stir well. Transfer the dressing to a 4-quart ovenproof casserole dish, cover, and bake until well browned and bubbly, about 45 minutes.

No Sugar Added Cranberry Relish

1 navel orange
2 cups fresh cranberries
¼ cup no sugar added orange marmalade

Leaving the peel intact, quarter and seed the orange. Place in a food processor, along with the cranberries and marmalade. Pulse to finely chop. Cover and chill in the refrigerator for 1 hour before serving.

Sugar Busters! Quick & Easy Cookbook

Fresh Green Bean and Pimiento Bundles

2 cups water

Dark green tops of 6 large green onions, halved
   lengthwise

1½ pounds fresh green beans, ends snapped

One 12-ounce jar pimientos or roasted red
   peppers, drained and cut into ¼-inch-thick
   strips

In a large skillet, bring the water to a simmer
over medium heat. Add the green onion tops
and cook just to soften, about 10 seconds. Remove with a slotted spoon and reduce the heat
to low. To make 12 bundles, tie 8 green beans
and 3 pimiento or roasted red pepper strips together with a green onion top. Place the bundles
in the water, raise the heat to medium-low, and
cover. Cook until the beans are crisp tender and
bright green, about 5 minutes.

Holiday Menus

Green Peas with Tiny Pearl Onions

3 tablespoons olive oil
3 tablespoons stone-ground whole-wheat flour
½ teaspoon dried thyme
2½ cups light cream
Two 1-pound packages frozen peas with pearl
   onions, thawed

Combine the oil and flour in a large saucepan
over medium heat. Whisking constantly, cook
for 1 minute. Add the thyme. Slowly whisk in
the cream and bring to a boil. Stir in the vegetables, cover, and cook for 2 to 3 minutes to heat
through.

Christmas Dinner for 8

Pork Roast prepared Cajun Pot Roast Style
(recipe follows)

Sautéed Mushrooms
(double recipe)
(see page 258)

Sassy Spinach Stuffed Tomatoes
(see page 275)

Instant Asparagus with Hollandaise Sauce
(double recipe)
(see page 219) (see page 317)

*Mixed Green Salad with Grapes and
Blue Cheese Dressing*
(recipe follows)

Whole-Grain Rolls
(recipe follows)

*SUGAR BUSTERS! Chocolate Mousse
from the kitchen of the Windsor Court Hotel
from SUGAR BUSTERS! Cut Sugar to Trim Fat,*
page 238

Pork Roast prepared Cajun Pot Roast Style

One 3-pound pork loin roast
1 cup Wish-Bone or other Italian salad dressing
2 tablespoons olive oil
½ teaspoon ground black pepper
½ cup dry white wine

Combine the roast and the salad dressing in a large plastic storage bag. Squeeze out excess air, seal tightly, and massage to coat the meat all over. Marinate in the refrigerator for at least 2 hours and up to overnight, turning the roast over at least once. Preheat a heavy Dutch oven over high heat. Add the oil. Remove the roast from the marinade and add it to the pan. Brown on all sides, 4 to 5 minutes. Pour the fat from the pan, and sprinkle the meat with the pepper. Add the wine. Cover, reduce heat to low, and cook until very tender, 2 to 2½ hours. Remove to a cutting board, cover with aluminum foil, and allow to sit for 10 minutes before thinly slicing.

Mixed Green Salad with Grapes and Blue Cheese Dressing

Two 4-ounce bags mixed baby greens
1 pound seedless red grapes
1 cup pecan halves
1¼ cups Blue Cheese Dressing (page 308)

In a salad bowl, combine the greens, grapes, and pecan halves. Mix, add the dressing, and toss to coat.

Whole-Grain Rolls

2¾ cups stone-ground whole-wheat flour
1 teaspoon salt
1 packet quick-rise yeast
⅓ cup olive oil
¾ cup plus 2 tablespoons water

Combine the flour, salt, and yeast in a food processor. Turn the machine on and process for 1 minute to blend. With the machine running, add the olive oil through the feed tube, then slowly add water just until a dough ball forms. (You may not need to use the full amount.) Continue to process for 30 seconds more to knead. Transfer the dough ball to a large, lightly greased bowl, cover with plastic wrap, and set aside until doubled in size, about 1 hour. Divide the dough into 8 equal pieces and form each into a ball. Place about 2 inches apart on a nonstick baking sheet. Cover loosely and set aside for about 45 minutes, until doubled. Preheat the oven to 400 degrees. Brush the top of each roll with olive oil and bake until browned and crusty, about 20 minutes.

Hanukkah Dinner for 8

Beef Brisket prepared Cajun Pot Roast Style
(recipe follows)

Sweet Potato Pancakes
(recipe follows)

Smothered Eggplant
(see page 250)

Broiled Tomatoes
(see page 280)

Cool Cabbage
(double recipe)
(see page 244)

Raspberries and Cream
from *SUGAR BUSTERS! Cut Sugar to Trim Fat,*
page 197

Beef Brisket prepared Cajun Pot Roast Style

One 3½-pound thin-cut beef brisket, trimmed
1½ cups Wish-Bone or other Italian salad
    dressing
2 tablespoons olive oil
¼ teaspoon ground black pepper
½ cup water

Combine the brisket and the salad dressing in a
large plastic storage bag. Squeeze out excess air,
seal tightly, and massage to coat the meat all
over. Marinate in the refrigerator for at least
2 hours and up to overnight, turning the brisket
over at least once. Preheat a large skillet over
high heat. Add the oil. Remove the meat from
the marinade and add it to the pan. Brown on
both sides, 3 to 4 minutes. Sprinkle with the
pepper. Add the water. Cover, reduce heat to
low, and cook until very tender, 2½ to 3 hours.
Remove to a cutting board and allow to sit for
10 minutes before thinly slicing across the grain.

Sweet Potato Pancakes

1 large sweet potato, scrubbed
½ teaspoon fresh lemon juice
1 tablespoon stone-ground whole-wheat flour
1 large egg, beaten
½ teaspoon seasoned salt
⅛ teaspoon ground white pepper
Pinch of baking soda
2 tablespoons olive oil

Peel and grate the sweet potato into a large bowl. Toss with the lemon juice. Stir in the flour, egg, seasoned salt, white pepper, and baking soda. Heat the olive oil in a large nonstick skillet over medium heat. Using ¼ cup of the batter for each, drop the pancakes in batches into the skillet, flattening each with a spatula. Cook until well browned, about 5 minutes a side.

New Year's Day Dinner for 6

Sautéed Oysters
(see page 190)

Italian Artichoke Soup
(see page 123)

Grilled Cornish Hens
(recipe follows)

Blackeyed Peas (for luck)
(see page 264)

Holiday Cabbage (for wealth)
(recipe follows)

Low-Sugar Lemon Crêpes
(see page 342)

Grilled Cornish Hens

¾ cup canola oil
½ cup fresh lemon juice
8 cloves garlic, minced
3 Rock Cornish hens, halved
Salt and ground black pepper to taste

In a small bowl, whisk the oil and lemon juice until well blended. Stir in the garlic and pour the mixture into a large plastic storage bag. Add the hens. Squeeze out excess air, seal tightly, and massage to coat the meat all over. Marinate in the refrigerator for 2 to 4 hours, turning once or twice. Preheat the broiler. Remove the hens from the marinade and place them skin side down on a broiler tray. Position 3 to 4 inches from the heat source, and broil for 13 minutes. Turn the hens over, season with salt and pepper, and broil until the birds are cooked through and the juices run clear, about 12 minutes.

Holiday Cabbage

2 quarts (8 cups) plus ½ cup water

1 teaspoon salt plus additional to taste

1 head green cabbage, shredded

3 strips bacon

1 medium white onion, chopped

6 cloves garlic, chopped

1 teaspoon balsamic vinegar

Bring the 2 quarts water to a boil in a Dutch oven. Stir in 1 teaspoon salt and the cabbage. Boil for 7 minutes, drain, and set aside. In a large skillet, fry the bacon until crisp over medium heat, 6 to 8 minutes. Remove to paper towels to drain. Add the onion, garlic, vinegar, and the remaining ½ cup water to the skillet. Stirring constantly, cook until the onion turns translucent, 2 to 3 minutes. Add the cabbage and crumble in the bacon. Stir to combine and cook until most of the water has evaporated, about 4 minutes. Add salt to taste.

Easter Supper for 8

Baked Ham with Ginger-Apricot Glaze
(recipe follows)

Steamed Artichokes
(quadruple recipe)
(see page 217)

Deviled Eggs
(double recipe)
(see page 296)

Turnip Greens
(double recipe)
(see page 256)

SUGAR BUSTERS! Salad
from the kitchen of the Palace Cafe
SUGAR BUSTERS! Cut Sugar to Trim Fat,
page 232

Sweet Potato Pecan Balls
(double recipe)
(see page 338)

Holiday Menus

Baked Ham with Ginger-Apricot Glaze

One 5-pound fully cooked ham
¾ cup no sugar added apricot fruit spread
1 tablespoon grated ginger
1 tablespoon Dijon mustard
½ tablespoon dry mustard

Preheat the oven to 325 degrees. Make cross-hatch slashes across the top of the ham with the tip of a knife. Place in a roasting pan. Bake for 30 minutes. Put the fruit spread into a small bowl. Stir in the ginger, Dijon mustard, and dry mustard. Spoon the glaze over the ham and bake until heated through, 20 to 30 minutes more. Remove to a cutting board, cover with aluminum foil, and let sit for 10 minutes before slicing.

Passover Seder for 8

Stuffed Bell Peppers
(recipe follows)

Steamed Cauliflower
(double recipe)
(see page 249)

Garlic Green Beans
(double recipe)
(see page 223)

Lentils
(see page 235)

Marinated Vegetables
(double recipe)
(see page 282)

Dessert Pecans
(see page 337)

Holiday Menus

Stuffed Bell Peppers

8 medium green bell peppers

2 tablespoons canola oil

2 pounds ground beef sirloin

1 large yellow onion, chopped

2 tablespoons minced fresh parsley

3 cloves garlic, finely chopped

1 teaspoon dried thyme

1 teaspoon dried basil

2 teaspoons salt

1 teaspoon freshly ground black pepper

¼ teaspoon cayenne pepper

2 tablespoons Worcestershire sauce

Two 28-ounce cans diced tomatoes, drained

One 29-ounce can tomato sauce

Preheat the oven to 400 degrees. Slice the tops off the bell peppers. Seed, core, rinse under cold running water, and set aside. Combine the oil, beef, and onion in a large, heavy skillet over medium heat. Stirring constantly, cook until the meat is no longer pink. Add the parsley, garlic, thyme, basil, salt, black pepper, cayenne pepper, and Worcestershire sauce. Still stirring, cook for about 3 minutes. Add the tomatoes and cook and stir for 5 minutes more to heat through. Stuff the peppers with the mixture and place them in a 9-by-12-inch baking dish. Pour the tomato sauce over the peppers. Cover with foil and bake until the peppers are soft and tender, about 30 minutes. Remove the foil and bake for 5 to 10 minutes more, until browned on top.

Summer Holiday Barbecue for 6 to 8

Texas Steak
(see page 203)

Crab Salad
(see page 100)

Fourth of July Macaroni Salad
(double recipe)
(see page 113)

Pinto Beans and Salsa
(see page 240)
(see page 320)

Fried Okra
(double recipe)
(see page 261)

*Vanilla Ice Cream with Blueberries and
Sliced Strawberries*
(recipe follows)

Vanilla Ice Cream with Blueberries and Sliced Strawberries

1 pint strawberries, rinsed
1 pint blueberries, rinsed and picked over
2 quarts Vanilla Ice Cream (page 340)

Hull and slice the strawberries. Put in a bowl and mix with the blueberries. Spoon over servings of ice cream.

XIII | Setting the Record Straight

We want to offer facts for all those who have had great success with the SUGAR BUSTERS! lifestyle or those who have or will consider following this lifestyle but have been confused by some of the statements made in the various media. Legitimate criticisms are always welcome concerning anything contained in our books, since we wish to establish a very credible dialogue regarding SUGAR BUSTERS!. We do not understand, however, statements made or written that are absolutely not factual or, at best, grossly misleading.

While flattered by the wide coverage SUGAR BUSTERS! has received, it is distressing to find that there are many out there who either have not read the book, or worse, are making or perpetuating statements that are simply not true. We will leave it to the readers of this book to judge what motives might persuade a non-technical writer or a spokesperson for an association to make such statements. It is interesting that the writers or spokespersons never call us to check on the accuracy of the statements they obtain from their customary, and in this case, often biased sources.

While many familiar with the SUGAR BUST-ERS! lifestyle can recognize such charges for what interests they represent, there are others who have no way of knowing what is true from what is false. For anyone somewhat confused, the following charges and facts are offered.

1) *The Charge:* "SUGAR BUSTERS! is just another low-calorie diet, only 800 to 1,000 calories a day."

The Facts: This is an absolutely false statement, and demonstrates the intent to mislead or a total lack of knowledge of what is in the book. Per rigorous analysis following prevalent nutrition industry guidelines, the 14-day meal plan averages 1,719 calories a day with no day as little as 1,000 calories. Also, the book states multiple times that (within reason) calories do not count, but, more importantly, the blood sugar–elevating potential (glycemic index) of carbohydrates is a better determinant of weight gain or loss.

2) *The Charge:* "SUGAR BUSTERS! is a low-carbohydrate diet that eliminates sugar."
The Facts: This statement also demonstrates a significant lack of knowledge by the individual making such a charge. The 14-day meal plan averages approximately 40 percent carbohydrates (sugar). Any doctor in America will tell you that carbohydrates are basically sugar. Only the unknowledgeable or uninformed would make such a statement. Regarding the 40 percent average, we believe you can consume even more carbohydrates, 50 to 55 percent, and not gain weight, if you simply choose the correct high-fiber, low-glycemic carbohydrates.

3) *The Charge:* "SUGAR BUSTERS! is a low-fiber diet."

The Facts: This charge is off by 180 degrees. SUGAR BUSTERS! strongly advocates eliminating low-fiber carbohydrates like refined sugars, white rice, and white flour products that have little or no fiber, while advocating the consumption of high-fiber, low-glycemic carbohydrates. Anyone who has read the book would never make such a statement. Of course, there is not enough original investigative journalism today, thus many myths are passed on by those who do no homework to verify the accuracy of the material or the credentials or apparent motivations of the people they quote.

4) *The Charge:* "You can only get diabetes through heredity; sugar does not cause diabetes."

The Facts: An extensive, six-year study on 65,173 healthy women by Dr. Jorge Salmaron, et al., as reported in the *Journal of the American Medical Association* in February 1997, determined that women who ate a high-glycemic, low-fiber diet developed diabetes at two and one half times the rate of women who ate a low-glycemic, high-fiber

diet. The latter is *exactly* what SUGAR BUST-
ERS! recommends. The report further con-
cluded that highly refined carbohydrates are
not as good for you as whole-grain carbohydrates when it comes to the likelihood of
developing diabetes. Since whole-grain, less-
processed carbohydrates are found to be better for you than refined sugars, you must
conclude, as did the extensive medical study,
that excessive consumption of refined carbohydrates (sugars) leads to an increased incidence of adult onset diabetes.

5) *The Charge:* "Everyone knows sugar does not
turn to fat; it is fat that turns to fat."
The Facts: Such a statement by a dietitian
and a spokesperson for the dietetic associa-
tion(s) clearly demonstrates the lack of knowledge of many (by no means all) dietitians or
nutritionists regarding basic medical textbook
facts. The *Textbook of Medical Physiology* by
Dr. Arthur C. Guyton clearly states that carbohydrates not needed for immediate energy
or stored as glycogen are converted to fat and
stored in the fat cells. Some nutritionists see
fat, think fat, smell fat, taste fat, and wrongly

assume that most of the fat on your body comes from fat. However, most of the fat on your body really comes from the carbohydrates you eat, not the fat. Since the diets recommended by most nutritionists over the last 25 years have been high-carbohydrate diets, is it any wonder Americans have gotten fatter and fatter (and more diabetic)!

6) *The Charge:* "SUGAR BUSTERS! is an unhealthy diet; it cuts out entire food groups."
The Facts: Since the diet recommended in the SUGAR BUSTERS! lifestyle is loaded with nutritious high-fiber vegetables, fruits, whole-grain products, dairy products, and lean meats of all varieties, we just cannot seem to figure what we have left out! If the writer of this charge, who could not have read the book, is talking about the highly processed and fiberless refined sugars (which are not a "food group"), we are happy we have recommended a minimum intake of these items.

Any vitamins and minerals present in the few excluded carbohydrates are easily replaced by eating the host of other carbohydrates that are recommended by the Sugar Busters! lifestyle. However, if you happen to be a "picky" consumer of vegetables, you can take a multi-vitamin each day to ensure an adequate intake of vitamins and minerals. You must be careful, however, to eat an adequate amount of carbohydrates and their associated fiber or you become ketotic (a state of acidosis) which is bad for your kidneys, muscles, and heart.

7) *The Charge:* "Well, SUGAR BUSTERS! may cause some weight loss initially, but it certainly will not work long-term."

The Facts: For hundreds of people who have communicated directly with us since 1995, we know this lifestyle works long-term. It has worked for three to six plus years for us, the authors of SUGAR BUSTERS! In spite of our increasing caloric intake, our blood cholesterol levels have decreased. Countless people have told us this is the only diet they have ever tried that not only takes the weight off but also keeps the weight off; all this without feeling deprived of good, nutritious food.

Index

Alcoholic Beverages
  acceptable, 25
  Bloody Mary Concentrate,
    290
Almonds, Trout Amandine,
  173–74
Appetizers. *See* Hors d'oeuvres
Apples
  Goochi, 335
  Patties, Browned (BAPS), 334
Apricot Glaze, -Ginger, with
  Baked Ham, 365
Artichokes
  Eggs Sardou, 67–68
  Soup, Italian, 123–24
  Steamed, 217–18
Asparagus, Instant, 219
Avocado
  Easy, 220
  Guacamole Salad, 106–7
  Soup, Chunky, No-Cook,
    125–26

Bacon
  Eggs Benedict, 65–66
  Spinach Salad, Fresh, with,
    119
Bagel and Cream Cheese, 62
Balsamic
  Broccoli, 243
  Vinaigrette, 313
BAPS (Browned Apple
  Patties), 334

Beans
  about, 25–27
  Chili, Meatless, 188–89
  Chili, Quick, 167
  glycemic index, 7, 26
  Kidney, with Ham, 233–34
  Lima, 237
  Lima, in Sour Cream,
    238–39
  Pinto, 240
  spices/herbs/seasonings,
    40–41
  White, 241–42
  White, -Garlic Soup, 131
  See also Black Beans; Green
    Beans; Lentils
Béarnaise Sauce, 315–16
Beef
  Bell Peppers, Stuffed, 367–68
  Brisket Cajun Pot Roast
    Style, 359
  Burger, Horseradish, 176
  Burgers, Lawry, 109
  Cabbage Patch Supper,
    157–58
  Chili, Quick, 167
  Fajitas, 168–69
  Flank Steak, 199–200
  Hamburger Steak, 175
  Omelet, Tidbit, 73–74
  Pot Roast, Cajun, 159–60
  Round Steak, Smothered,
    202

Sirloins, Ginger Marinated, 201
spices/herbs/seasonings, 38–39, 40
Stock, 327
Texas Steak, 203–4
Bell Peppers
  Stuffed, 367–68
  Western Omelet, 84–85
Beverages
  acceptable, 25, 57–58, 87
  liquid consumption, 14–15
Black Beans
  Dieter's Delight, 221–22
  Soup, Quick-Draw, 127–28
  Soup, Traditional, 129–30
Blackeyed Peas, 264–65
Blood sugar, 2, 3, 4
Bloody Mary Concentrate, 290
Blueberries, Vanilla Ice Cream with Sliced Strawberries and, 370
Blue Cheese Dressing, 308
  Mixed Green Salad with Grapes and, 356
Breads
  acceptable, 22
  Bagel and Cream Cheese, 62
  glycemic index, 4–6
  Rolls, Whole-Grain, 357
  See also Toast
Brisket Cajun Pot Roast Style, 359
Broccoli
  Balsamic, 243
  Mock Oysters, 300
Broths, basic, 28–29, 327
Brown Rice. See Rice, Brown
Burgers
  Flank Steak, 199–200
  Hamburger Steak, 175

Horseradish, 176
Lawry, 109

Cabbage
  Holiday, 363
  Patch Supper, 157–58
  Sweet and Sour, 247–48
  See also Slaw
Caesar Salad
  Chicken, 94
  Dressing, 307
Cajun Pot Roast, 159–60
  Beef Brisket, 359
  Pork, 355
Calories, 13–14, 372–73
Carbohydrates, 373, 375
  and glycemic index, 3–9
  -protein-fat ratio, 12
Cauliflower, Steamed, 249
Cereals
  acceptable, 24, 63
  glycemic index, 4–6
  Oatmeal, Hearty, 72
Ceviche, 291–92
Cheese
  Dip, Con Queso, 293
  Enchiladas, and Chicken, 161–62
  Green Chilies Casserole, 105
  Lasagna, Spinach, 183–84
  Omelet, and Green Onion, 64
  Roquefort Dressing, 312
  Spread, and Tuna, 303
  Squash Con Queso, 273
  See also Blue Cheese Dressing
Cherry Tomatoes and Prosciutto, 302
Chestnut and Green Bean Casserole, 225–26
Chicken
  Caesar Salad, 94

Chicken *(cont'd)*
Curried, on Brown Rice,
163–64
Enchiladas, and Cheese,
161–62
Ginger, Stir-Fried, 95–96
Grilled, Oriental, 166
Mexicano, 93
Omelet, Tidbit, 73–74
Orange Ginger, 165
Salad, Tarragon, 97
Soup, Simple, 135
Soup with Tomatoes and
Green Beans, 133–34
spices/herbs/seasonings,
39
Stock, 28–29, 327
Chili
Meatless, 188–89
Quick, 167
Chilies, Green
Cheese Casserole, 105
Chicken Mexicano, 93
Eggs (Huevos) with Salsa,
Spicy, 79–80
Omelet, Spanish, Savory,
77–78
Soup, and Jalapeño, 140–41
Soup, Tortillaless, 146–47
-Squash Casserole, 270
Christmas dinner, 354–57
Cider Vinaigrette, 314
Cole Slaw. *See* Slaw
Condiments
acceptable, 22–23
Cranberry Relish, No Sugar
Added, 351
Cornish Hens, Grilled, 362
Crab
Cakes, Chesapeake, 98–99
Dip, 294
Eggplant, Stuffed, 251–52
Salad, 100

Cranberry Relish, No Sugar
Added, 351
Creole Spinach, 274
Crêpes, Lemon, Low-Sugar,
342–44
Cucumber and Tomato Soup,
Cool, 144–45
Curry(ied)
Chicken on Brown Rice,
163–64
Dip, Vegetable, 295
Lamb, 178–79
Rice, 269
Custard, Egg, 336

Dairy products
acceptable, 21–22
glycemic index, 9
spices/herbs/seasonings, 44
Desserts, 331–32
BAPS (Browned Apple
Patties), 334
Crêpes, Lemon, Low-Sugar,
342–44
Custard, Egg, 336
Goochi Apples, 335
Pecans, 337
Sweet Potato Pecan Balls,
338–39
See also Ice cream
Deviled Eggs, 296
Diabetes, 10, 11, 374–75
Dips
Con Queso, 293
Crab, 294
Curry Vegetable, 295
Dressing, Veal and Pork, with
Chopped Pecans, 349–50

Easter supper, 364–65
Eggplant
Smothered, 250
Stuffed, 251–52

Eggs
  Benedict, 65–66
  Custard, 336
  Deviled, 296
  French Toast, 81
  Green Chilies Cheese
    Casserole, 105
  with Grilled Tomatoes,
    75–76
  Huevos with Salsa, Spicy,
    79–80
  Salad in Tomato Shells,
    101–2
  Sardou, 67–68
  See also Omelets
Enchiladas, Chicken and
    Cheese, 161–62

Fajitas, 168–69
Fat, body, 375–76
Fat, dietary
  -carbohydrate-protein ratio,
    12
  oils, 29–31
  saturated, 12–13, 29, 56
Fettucine with "Raw"
    Tomato Sauce, 112
Fiber, 3–4, 373–74
Fish
  acceptable, 21
  Baked, Succulent, 171–72
  Ceviche, 291–92
  Fillets and Skillet
    Vegetables, 103–4
  Grilled, -Quick Skillet, 170
  Sauce, Hot, 319
  Sauce, Meunière, 321
  spices/herbs/seasonings, 40
  Stock, 327
  Trout Amandine, 173–74
  See also Salmon; Tuna
Flank Steak, 199–200
French Dressing, Quick, 309

French Onion Soup, 136–37
French Toast, 81
Fruits
  acceptable, 19–20
  glycemic index, 8
  spices/herbs/seasonings, 44
  and Yogurt, Fresh, 71
  See also specific fruits

Garlic
  Green Beans, 223
  Roasted, 253
  -White Bean Soup, 131–32
Gazpacho Soup, 138–39
Ginger
  -Apricot Glaze, with Baked
    Ham, 365
  Chicken, Orange, 165
  Chicken, Stir-Fried, 95–96
  Sirloins, Marinated, 201
Glycemic index, 3–9
Grains
  glycemic index, 4–6
  spices/herbs/seasonings, 44
Grapes, Green Salad, Mixed,
    with Blue Cheese
    Dressing and, 356
Gravy, Natural, with Turkey,
    347–48
Green Beans
  Casserole, Simple, 224
  and Chestnut Casserole,
    225–26
  Chicken Soup with
    Tomatoes and, 133–34
  Garlic, 223
  and Horseradish Sauce,
    227–28
  Italiano, 229–30
  with Mustard Sauce,
    231–32
  and Pimiento Bundles,
    Fresh, 352

Greens
 Salad, Mixed, with Grapes
  and Blue Cheese
  Dressing, 356
 Smothered, 254–55
 Turnip, 256–57
Green Tomatoes, Fried, 281
Guacamole Salad, 106–7

Ham
 Baked, with Ginger-Apricot
  Glaze, 365
 Cherry Tomatoes and
  Prosciutto, 302
 Eggs Benedict, 65–66
 with Kidney Beans, 233–34
 Western Omelet, 84–85
Hamburger Steak, 175
Hanukkah dinner, 358–60
Herbs, 38–55
 Lamb, -Crusted, 180
Hollandaise Sauce, 317–18
Hors d'oeuvres
 Ceviche, 291–92
 Cherry Tomatoes and
  Prosciutto, 302
 Deviled Eggs, 296
 Oyster Ramakis, 297
 Oysters, Mock, 300
 Oysters, Spicy, 301
 Oysters Tony, 298–99
 Tuna and Cheese Spread,
  303
 See also Dips
Horseradish
 Burger, 176
 Sauce, and Green Beans,
  227
 Spinach, Spicy, 279

Ice cream
 glycemic index, 9
 Vanilla, 340–41

Vanilla, with Blueberries
 and Sliced Strawberries,
 370
Insulin, 2, 14

Jalapeño
 and Green Chili Soup,
  140–41
 Tortillaless Soup, 146–47

Kidney Beans with Ham,
 233–34

Lamb
 Chops, Broiled, 177
 Curried, 178–79
 Herb-Crusted, 180
 Omelet, Tidbit, 73–74
 spices/herbs/seasonings, 39
 Stew, 181–82
Lasagna
 Mexican, 186–87
 Spinach, 183–84
Lawry Burgers, 109
Lemon
 Crêpes, Low-Sugar, 342–44
 Veal Piccata, 208–9
Lentils, 235
 Salad, Chilled, 108
 Spicy, 236
Lima Beans, 237
 in Sour Cream, 238–39

Macaroni Salad, Fourth of
 July, 113
Marinara Sauce, 320
Meats
 acceptable, 20–21
 roasts, 27–28
 See also specific meats
Meunière Sauce, 321
Mexican Lasagna, 186–87
Mushrooms

Mock Oysters, 300
  Sautéed, 258
Mustard
  Dressing, -Based, 310
  Eggs, Deviled, 296
  Pork, Roast, with, 193
  Sauce, Green Beans with,
    231–32
Mustard Greens, Smothered,
  254–55

New Year's Day dinner,
  361–63
Nuts
  glycemic index, 9
  snacks, 332
  Trout Amandine, 173–74
  See also Pecans

Oatmeal, Hearty, 72
Obesity, in children, 11–12
Oils, about, 29–30
Okra
  Fried, 261
  Smothered, 262
  and Tomatoes, 259–60
Olive-Tomato Sauce, with
  Whole-Wheat Spaghetti,
  110–11
Omelets
  Cheese and Green Onion, 64
  Florentine (Spinach), 69–70
  Spanish, Savory, 77–78
  Tidbit, 73–74
  Western, 84–85
Onions
  Green, and Cream Cheese
    Omelet, 64
  Pearl, Tiny, with Green
    Peas, 353
  Soup, French, 136–37
Orange Chicken, Ginger, 165
Oriental Chicken, Grilled, 166

Oysters
  Mock, 300
  Ramakis, 297
  Sautéed, 190
  Spicy, 301
  Tony, 298–99

Pancakes, Sweet Potato, 360
Passover Seder, 366–68
Pasta
  acceptable, 24
  Fettucine with "Raw"
    Tomato Sauce, 112
  glycemic index, 5, 6
  Lasagna, Spinach, 183–84
  Macaroni Salad, Fourth of
    July, 113
  Spaghetti, Whole-Wheat,
    with Olive-Tomato
    Sauce, 110–11
Pasta Sauces
  Basic, 322
  Marinara, 320
  Tomato, Basic, 325–26
Peas
  Blackeyed, 264–65
  Green, with Tiny Pearl
    Onions, 353
Pecans
  Chopped, with Veal and
    Pork Dressing, 349–50
  Dessert, 337
  Sweet Potato Balls, 338–39
Peppers. *See* Chilies, Green;
  Jalapeño; Bell Peppers
Pinto Beans, 240
Pork
  Dressing, and Veal, with
    Chopped Pecans, 349–50
  Lasagna, Mexican, 186–87
  Roast Cajun Pot Roast
    Style, 355
  Roast, with Mustard, 193

Pork *(cont'd)*
 spices/herbs/seasonings, 40
 Stuffed Loin, 194
 Tender, Grilled, 191–92
 See also Bacon; Ham
Portion size, 13–14
Pot Roast. *See* Cajun Pot Roast
Prosciutto and Cherry
  Tomatoes, 302
Protein-carbohydrate-fat ratio,
  12

Quail, Holiday Birds, 155–56

Ranch Dressing, 311
Red Cabbage, Sweet and Sour,
  247–48
Relish, Cranberry, No Sugar
  Added, 351
Remoulade Sauce, 323
Rice, Brown
 acceptable, 24
 Chicken Mexicano, 93
 Curried, 269
 Curried Chicken on,
  163–64
 Fried, 267–68
 glycemic index, 5, 6
Rolls, Whole-Grain, 357
Roquefort Dressing, 312

Salad Dressing
 Caesar, 307
 French, Quick, 309
 Mustard-Based, 310
 Ranch, 311
 Roquefort, 312
 See also Blue Cheese
  Dressing; Vinaigrette
Salads
 Caesar, Chicken, 94
 Chicken, Tarragon, 97
 Crab, 100

Egg, in Tomato Shells, 101–2
Green, Mixed, with Grapes
  and Blue Cheese
  Dressing, 356
Guacamole, 106–7
Lentil, Chilled, 108
Macaroni, Fourth of July,
  113
Shrimp, 118
Shrimp, Seared, 114
spices/herbs/seasonings, 45
Spinach, Fresh, with Bacon,
  119
Tuna, Blackened, 121–22
Tuna, Classic, 120
See also Slaw
Salmon
 Grilled, 195
 Poached, 196
Salsa, 324
 with Eggs (Huevos), Spicy,
  79–80
Sauces
 Béarnaise, 315–16
 Fish, Hot, 319
 Hollandaise, 317–18
 Horseradish, and Green
  Beans, 227–28
 Lemon Butter, 343–44
 Marinara, 320
 Meunière, 321
 Mustard, with Green Beans,
  231–32
 Olive-Tomato, with
  Whole-Wheat Spaghetti,
  110–11
 Pasta, Basic, 322
 Remoulade, 323
 spices/herbs/seasonings, 45
 Tomato, Basic, 325–26
Scallop and Shrimp
  "Goulash", 116–17
Seasonings, 38–55

Shellfish
  acceptable, 21
  Scallop and Shrimp
    "Goulash", 116–17
  spices/herbs/seasonings, 40
  See also Crab; Oysters;
    Shrimp
Shrimp
  Salad, 118
  Sautéed, 198–99
  and Scallop "Goulash",
    116–17
  Seared, Salad, 114
  Spicy Boiled, Bayou, 115
Sirloins, Ginger Marinated,
  201
Slaw
  Cool Cabbage, 244
  Creamy Cabbage, 245
  Sour Cream, 246
Snacks, 328–30
Soups
  Artichoke, Italian, 123–24
  Avocado, Chunky,
    No-Cook, 125–26
  Black Bean, Quick-Draw,
    127–28
  Black Bean, Traditional,
    129–30
  Chicken, Simple, 135
  Chicken, with Tomatoes
    and Green Beans,
    133–34
  Gazpacho, 138–39
  Green Chili and Jalapeño,
    140–41
  Onion, French, 136–37
  spices/herbs/seasonings,
    46–47
  Sweet Potato, 142–43
  Tomato and Cucumber,
    Cool, 144–45
  Tortillaless, 146–47

Sour Cream
  Cole Slaw, 246
  Lima Beans in, 238–39
Spaghetti, Whole-Wheat, with
  Olive-Tomato Sauce,
  110–11
Spanish Omelet, Savory,
  77–78
Spices, 36–37, 38–55
Spinach
  Creole, 274
  Eggs Sardou, 67–68
  Lasagna, 183–84
  Omelet, Florentine, 69–70
  Salad, Fresh, with Bacon,
    119
  Sautéed, 277–78
  Spicy, 279
  Tomatoes, Stuffed, Sassy,
    275–76
Squash
  Casserole, 272
  Con Queso, 273
  -Green Chili Casserole,
    270–71
Steak. *See* Beef
Stew, Lamb, 181–82
Stocks, basic, 28–29, 327
Strawberries, Sliced, Vanilla
  Ice Cream with
  Blueberries and, 370
Sweet Potato
  Baked, 266
  Pancakes, 360
  Pecan Balls, 338–39
Sweet Potato
  Soup, 142–43
Sweet and Sour Cabbage,
  247–48

Tarragon Chicken Salad, 97
Texas Steak, 203–4
Thanksgiving dinner, 346–53

Toast
  French Toast, 81
  Tasty, 83
Tomatoes
  Broiled, 280
  Cherry, and Prosciutto, 302
  Chicken Soup with Green
    Beans and, 133–34
  Egg Salad in Tomato Shells,
    101–2
  Gazpacho Soup, 138–39
  Green, Fried, 281
  Grilled, with Eggs, 75–76
  and Okra, 259–60
  Salsa, 324
  Soup, and Cucumber, Cool,
    144–45
  Spinach Stuffed, Sassy,
    275–76
  Veal Scaloppine with, 210–11
Tomato Sauce
  Basic, 325–26
  Marinara, 320
  Olive-, with Whole-Wheat
    Spaghetti, 110–11
  Pasta, Basic, 322
  "Raw", with Fettucine, 112
Tortillaless Soup, 146–47
Tortillas
  Enchiladas, Chicken and
    Cheese, 161–62
  Fajitas, 168–69
  Lasagna, Mexican, 186–87
Trout Amandine, 173–74
Tuna
  Blackened, Salad, 121–22
  and Cheese Spread, 303
  Salad, Classic, 120
Turkey
  with Natural Gravy, 347–48
  spices/herbs/seasonings, 40
  Supreme, 205–6
Turnip Greens, 256–57

Veal
  Chops, 212
  Dressing, and Pork, with
    Chopped Pecans,
    349–50
  Marsala, 207
  Piccata, 208–9
  Scaloppine with Tomatoes,
    210–11
  spices/herbs/seasonings,
    40
Vegetables
  acceptable, 18–19, 25–27
  Curry Dip, 295
  Gazpacho Soup, 138–39
  glycemic index, 7
  Marinated, 282
  Sautéed, 283–84
  Skillet, and Fish Fillets,
    103–4
  spices/herbs/seasonings,
    40–44
  See also specific
    vegetables
Venison, Smothered, 202
Vinaigrette
  Balsamic, 313
  Cider, 314
Vitamins and minerals,
  376–77

Water consumption, 14–15
Weight gain/loss, 10, 11, 14,
  373, 377
Western Omelet, 84–85
Wines, acceptable, 25

Yogurt, 9, 21–22
  and Fresh Fruit, 71

Zucchini
  Instant, 285
  Smothered, 286